# God and Public Relations Methods Make Church Renewal, Growth and Outreach Happen

## Never Underestimate the Power of God

Millennial Mind Publishing
An imprint of American Book Publishing
5442 So. 900 East, #146
Salt Lake City, UT 84117-7204
www.american-book.com
Printed in the United States of America on acid-free paper.

God and Public Relations Methods Make Church Renewal, Growth and Outreach Happen
Designed by Dimitar Bochukov, design@american-book.com

**Publisher's Note:** American Book Publishing relies on the author's integrity of research and attribution; each statement has not been investigated to determine if it has been accurately made. The author and publisher specifically disclaim any responsibility for any liability, loss, or risk, personal or otherwise, which is incurred as a consequence, directly or indirectly, of the use and application of any of the contents of this book. In such situations where medical, legal, or other professional services may apply, please seek the advice of such professionals directly.

ISBN-13: 978-1-58982-564-2
ISBN-10: 1-58982-564-0

Library of Congress Cataloging-in-Publication Data

Hayward, Richard B.
 God and public relations methods make church renewal, growth, and outreach happen : never underestimate the power of God / Richard B. Hayward.
    p. cm.
 ISBN-13: 978-1-58982-564-2
 ISBN-10: 1-58982-564-0
 1. Church public relations. 2. Church renewal. 3. Church growth. I. Title.
 BV653.H38 2009
 254'.4--dc22
                                    2009025017

**Special Sales:** These books are available at special discounts for bulk purchases. Special editions, including personalized covers, excerpts of existing books, and corporate imprints, can be created in large quantities for special needs. For more information e-mail info@american-book.com.

# God and Public Relations Methods Make Church Renewal, Growth and Outreach Happen

## *Never Underestimate the Power of God*

Richard B. Hayward

# Dedication

I am grateful to Betty Joe, my wonderful wife of fifty years, for her daily, positive way of enjoying life and her inspiration in the writing of this book.

I really appreciate all the thoughtful constructive suggestions of Edith Barron, Trudy Flenniken and Nancy Salama, the members of a monthly Christian Critique Group, as they shared their expertise to keep every chapter in the book clear, concise and focused on the message of the book.

I never knew how important an editor was in helping the language of a book flow in a readable manner, but I want to especially thank my editors and all the staff at American Book Publishing for helping to make it happen.

# Table of Contents

**Introduction** ........................................................................... 1

**A Preface** — What Does the Author Know about It? ...... 5

**Chapter One:** Prayer Is the Key to
Church, Renewal, Growth and Outreach ...................... 13

**Chapter Two:** Public Relations Begins
with the Pastor and a Positive Faith in God ................ 17

**Chapter Three:** Beginning the Process of Church
Renewal, Growth, and Outreach Using God's
Guidance and Public Relations Methods ...................... 21

**Chapter Four:** The First Action of the Church Board
Is to Plan a Public Relations Outreach Campaign ....... 25

**Chapter Five:** Raising Church Morale
and Hope for Church Renewal ..................................... 27

**Chapter Six:** Planning and Resources for
Church Renewal, Growth, and Outreach ...................... 31

**Chapter Seven:** Attracting New People
by Upgrading Facilities ................................................ 35

**Chapter Eight:** Creating Joyful, Meaningful
Worship Services to Attract Visitors ............................ 37

**Chapter Nine:** Beginning or Stimulating
a Sunday School ........................................................... 49

**Chapter Ten:** Junior Memberships
and Church Scholarships Keep Children and Youth
Interested in the Church .............................................. 55

**Chapter Eleven:** Making Adult Classes
Exciting and Meaningful ...........................................59
**Chapter Twelve:** Improving a Church's Image Using
Public Relations Methods .........................................63
**Chapter Thirteen:** Promoting a Church's Image
Using Newspapers, Magazines, Radio,
Television and the Internet.......................................71
**Chapter Fourteen:** Reaching the Unchurched
  in an Inexpensive, Minimum-Effort,
  Non-threatening Way..............................................85
**Chapter Fifteen:** Personalizing Funeral
  and Wedding Services ...........................................95
**Chapter Sixteen:** Suggestions to Help Create
  Happy Marriages...............................................103
**Chapter Seventeen:** Helping Young People
  with the Three Greatest Choices of Their Lives ....... 113
**Chapter Eighteen:** Effective Healing
  and Hospital Ministry Techniques...........................121
**Chapter Nineteen:** Getting a Church off of a Plateau....... 133
  *Appendix:* The How to Do It Dial Hope Manual ...... 139
  *About the Author*...............................................175

# Dedication

This book is dedicated to:

* the power and guidance of God who makes things happen in all churches;

* pastors, seminary students, part time pastors, men and women leaders, and churches struggling with the problems of church renewal, growth and outreach;

* the hope that some of the suggestions in this book will help churches with their ministry of reaching men and women who need the power of God to help them in their quests for lives of meaning, purpose, strength, peace and happiness beyond their dreams.

Although this book is copyrighted, permission is granted to pastors and churches to use and reproduce any part of this book for their ministry.

# Introduction

Most of the denominations in the United States have experienced a steady decline in membership over the past thirty years.

Why has this been happening?

What can be done to turn this trend around?

How can churches reach the unchurched in their communities?

In business, the answer to similar trends centers on ways to reach the target audience with improved products using information to convince long-time and potential customers to buy and use more of their products. The means of promoting the company is accomplished by using public relations methods that include positive messages about the company's products, planning activities to promote the products, and using the available media to reach the target audience.

This same method could be applied to a church with similar results.

This book is designed to assist pastors and members in experiencing a new vision of church renewal that is based on prayer and dedication to God.

After a career as an Air Force Chaplain and the fact

that there were 1200 more pastors than pulpits in my denomination when I retired, I had to find another career. I decided to take a year of graduate study in public relations, to become a Director of Public Relations for an organization.

During my ten years as an award winning professional Public Relations Director for all of the YMCAs of San Diego County, I used public relations methods to help the organization grow.

I am convinced that using these methods in a step by step manner can help any church with renewal, growth and outreach.

In 1988, a small church in a multi-cultural community of San Diego was scheduled to be closed by the denomination, and the members were told it would happen. They prayed for someone to help them. I was praying for some place to serve. God brought us together. No one told me that the church was to be closed, (I found out two years later.) I used public relations methods to help the church continue its mission. I retired after completing 20 years as their pastor.

In this book, I have suggested and described a step by step process that follows basic public relations methods as they apply to churches:

- studying the present church programs and activities;
- thinking about, and defining the desires and needs of a target group, which includes the members and friends of the church;
- using questionnaires from the members and friends for improving the different activities of the church;
- holding brainstorming conferences that include all the members of the church, using questionnaires

and suggestions of those present to improve the church programs;
- finding volunteers to form committees for action;
- raising the morale of the church members;
- initiating suggested improvements in the church program;
- planning to use the available media;
- getting suggestions for ways to create and implement outreach programs.

This book also includes some specific suggestions a church may or may not decide to use:

- raise church morale with a Heritage Weekend;
- use silent prayer as a method to focus on the church's mission and make things happen for individuals and the church;
- make a prayer group relevant;
- some suggestions about worship services;
- make Bible classes interesting with a minimum of leadership preparation;
- offer classes that meet personal and family needs to help attract new people to the church;
- make the church relevant for children and teenagers;
- improve the Sunday or church school with a minimum of leadership preparation;
- create a church public relations calendar that includes special events and recreational activities;
- create a non-threatening way of reaching anyone with personal needs 24/7 by using a recorded telephone ministry.

I have included many suggestions I used during my

fifty eight years as an ordained chaplain and pastor that may help pastors and churches.

I hope that this book will help pastors and churches with their renewal, growth, and outreach.

I want it clearly understood that the most important product of every church is complete faith in the power of God to lead individuals and churches in renewal, growth and outreach. Public relations methods are only a means to help make this happen. This book is about using faith in the power of God and public relations methods that have helped me in my ministry and I hope will assist other pastors and churches with their ministry.

# A Preface — What Does the Author Know about It?

Any time a person writes a book suggesting solutions to any problem in life, the reader wants to know the writer's background and experience that led him to write a book on the subject. The reader wants to know his personal experience about the subject in order to decide to accept or reject his suggestions.

I found out about the reality, power and guidance of God in my life one day during WWII as a rifleman on the frontlines. Our platoon was ordered to attack a machine gun nest on a hill. It was the most horrible experience of my life. After sporadic fire fights that lasted all day, our platoon went from 39 men to 13 men and our squad went from 13 men to three men and all of my buddies were gone. (Thankfully, most of them were only wounded.) I was all alone thousands of miles from home!

As night fell, I was shivering! I was cold to the bone! When would I be killed or wounded? Tomorrow? Next week? Next month? When? Fear and terror gripped my mind! I was shaking all over! My thoughts were racing! My head felt like it was bursting! I was sobbing! I fell to my knees and cried out, *"Oh God! I'm at the end of my rope! You take over! I'm your man whether I live, die or become wounded. Amen!"* I fell into a deep sleep. When I woke up, the sun was shining in my eyes and I was at peace. God was with me! I went on for another 119 days on and ahead of the frontlines. I wasn't afraid anymore. God was with me and has been with me ever since.

In Japan after the war, I was an innocent bystander facing a possible court-martial. I prayed asking God for someone to help me. I found the only person that could help me was a chaplain. (He could go to anyone in the company at any time to help me.) He said, "Don't worry, I'll take care of it." And he did! It was then that I decided to become a chaplain in order to help other men and women in the Armed Forces.

After my discharge from the Army, I faced four years of college and three years of seminary to become a chaplain. I didn't have financial help from my parents or any other source of income except for three years from the G.I. Bill. I prayed asking God for guidance and a job. I got a full time newspaper distribution job. I attended the University of Southern California mornings and worked in the afternoons, driving 100 miles a day.

When I was 24 years old, I decided that I needed a special lady to be a chaplain's wife. I prayed and God guided me to a church with a large college-age young people's group where I met Betty Joe. After a thirteen month courtship, we were married. We went to San Francisco Theological Seminary. Again I prayed for jobs to put me through seminary and Betty through college. I got two part time jobs and preached at a student pastorate 40 miles from the seminary on Sundays. This income, plus the G.I. Bill, put us both through school. Betty drove fifty miles a day, including a ferry boat ride, to the University of California. We both graduated debt free from our schools during the same month in 1953.

I was commissioned an Air Force Chaplain.

All through my Air Force chaplaincy career, God's leading power caused amazing things to happen on every base.

On my first base, Langley Air Force Base, Virginia, I was duty chaplain. One night, the hospital called and told me a sergeant's mother wasn't expected to live through the night, and the immediate family had gathered to support each other through her final moments. I drove to the hospital, read comforting scriptures and prayed with the family. Since this took place in the room where the beloved mother lay in a coma under an oxygen tent, I thought I should pray for the mother. Her hand lay on the covers. I took her hand and prayed aloud for her healing. Then I gave the family my card for future use and left.

One week later I was visiting patients in the hospital. I came to the room where I had prayed with the mother and her family. I wondered who had replaced her. I walked in the room and said, *"I'm Chaplain Hayward,"* The woman looked up at me and said, *"You're the chaplain who prayed for me. I was in a coma but I heard your prayer and I'm going to get well."* She completely recovered and attended my chapel services for the next year. I was amazed that my prayer was answered, and from that time on, I always prayed for healing even with the terminally ill, with some amazing results. Years later as a pastor; a doctor told a family of a senior lady that because of her age she probably would not survive a serious operation. One of her sons asked me to pray for her. One day before going to the hospital, I visited her in her home and prayed with her for a successful operation. After a successful operation, a nurse asked her if she wanted any pain pills. She said "I don't have any pain." She completely recovered and continued attending church services for another five years.

Another amazing happening occurred when I sat next to a lady during a dull meeting and I gave her a copy of an article I had written at the request of a national chaplain's organization for a book summarizing retired chaplain's careers. She read about my praying for a mother in a coma expected to die. When the meeting adjourned, she asked me to pray for her. We stepped aside and I asked her "What do you want me to pray for?" She said, "My eyes." I took her hands and prayed for the healing of her eyes. I got her name and address to send her some helpful prayers and materials. She thanked me. A week later I received a letter from her. She had had a complete examination of her eyes and the doctor told her she wasn't going blind. A month earlier a doctor told her she was going to become blind due to diabetes. Four years later she still has her eye sight. Needless to say I believe in the power of prayer and never underestimate the power of God.

During my chaplaincy career, two years following my experience on Langley Air Force Base, I was assigned to a Fighter Day Squadron that was transferred from England to Soesterberg Air Base in The Netherlands. One of my official duties was to hold a Sunday Service on the last Sunday of each month for the Embassy, Military Assistance Group and other Americans in The Hague, forty-five miles away. This meant that on that Sunday I could not hold a service on the base.

An officer of the MAAG Group was a voluntary Sunday School Superintendent for about seventy-five children every Sunday in The Hague. About eighty people attended the once a month Sunday Service. At a

Sunday School teacher training meeting, a lady suggested that perhaps they could found an American civilian church in The Hague with a civilian pastor.

I thought this was a good idea and at the next monthly service, I asked that anyone interested in founding an American Protestant Church in The Hague come to the front of the Hospital Chapel after the service. After the service, I went to the entrance of the chapel to greet the people as they left. They all seemed to be leaving.

Only ten people were sitting on the front row; an Air Force Colonel, some officials from the Embassy, and an oil company executive. The colonel said, *"Well, Chaplain, you can see there isn't enough interest in forming a church. Let's forget it."* I thought back to the seminary student pastorate I served for two and a half years with its 24 members and an average Sunday Service attendance of 13. I remembered what those ordinary people had done. Then I looked at the caliber of the people on the front row. I said, *"I think we should pray about this for a month and see what God says."*

I had someone find out how many Americans lived in The Hague. Then I sent a letter to the National Council of Churches, Overseas Churches Department, asking how to found an overseas church.

*Now see how God works!* My letter arrived on the desk of the Director of the 92 overseas churches at the same time a letter from Dr. Bremicker, a Presbyterian pastor with 25 years experience. Dr. Bremicker's letter stated that he and his wife wanted to help a church in Europe for a few years. He would pay his and his wife's passage to and from Europe. Their only request was that the church provide them with an apartment, a stipend for food and utilities, and no salary.

The Overseas Director was planning an around the

world trip to visit American Churches. His first stop would be The Hague. He met with our organizing committee and told us what to do.

One year later, I installed Dr. Bremicker as the first pastor of the <u>American Protestant Church of The Hague</u>. In a few years the Church grew to five hundred members.

Think about this and about how God works. If I had not had the experience of my student pastorate, I probably would have agreed with the colonel and the American Protestant Church in The Hague would not have been founded.

I was guest founding pastor during their 50th Anniversary in 2006. The church building was designated as a National Treasure of The Netherlands, and they received $100,000 from the government to keep the building in mint condition.

*Never underestimate the power of God!*

My next assignment was Manzano Air Base, a top secret base located in the desert ten miles from Sandia Army Base in Albuquerque, New Mexico. Only the men and families assigned to the base were allowed on the base and the families lived on Sandia Army Base.

In order for the families to attend Sunday Services, they had to drive past a huge Army chapel and travel ten miles into the desert to the Manzano Base. My problem was how could we reach anyone who was not assigned to the base for God? I asked the small congregation to pray for some way that we could reach people beyond the base.

The answer came: a taped radio program over a commercial radio station. We didn't have the money for the project, but there were two large bases in Albuquerque; Sandia Army Base and Kirtland Air Force Base. They could supply the funds and then each base could be featured every third month.

I went to a three day radio workshop in Tulsa, Oklahoma to find out how to create a taped program for radio. I got funds from the Chief of Chaplains for an organist and a choir director. The Choir Director, along with three buddies, formed a barbershop quartet for music.

To find out the cost before I approached the base chaplains at Sandia and Kirtland, I went to the third largest radio station in Albuquerque and explained to the manager my plan for a thirty minute weekly taped Sunday Service of music and a message. I explained how I went to a radio workshop to find out how to do it.

After I finished my presentation, the manager said, "If you promise that you will not tell anyone about this, I will give you thirty minutes every Sunday morning from 10:00 to 10:30 a.m. for $10 a Sunday."

I couldn't believe it! I agreed. I didn't say anything to the two base chaplains, and for two years we had a taped radio broadcast over the third largest radio station in Albuquerque every Sunday. We received letters of appreciation from ranchers, townspeople and college students all over New Mexico.

*Never underestimate the power of God!*

God's guidance led me to do amazing things, to reach the unchurched on every base. During my Air Force career, I baptized and connected 355 adults to local churches.

After my retirement from the Air Force, there were 1200 more ministers than pastorates in my denominational church. I completed a year of graduate study in Public Relations and became a Public Relations Director for all of the YMCAs in San Diego County for ten years. During one of those years I won an award for the Outstanding Publicity Campaign in San Diego County in competition with 50 public relations professionals. Then I became a Chaplain-Counselor for recovering alcoholics in the Salvation Army Adult Rehabilitation Center of San Diego for six years.

In 1988, I became pastor of a church that was scheduled to be closed by the denomination. The members were told it would happen. The members began praying for someone to help them. I was praying for some place to serve in a church. God brought us together, but no one told me the church was to be closed. (I found out two years later.) Using prayer, my public relations experience and God's help, I was able to help the church continue helping people to experience God in their lives and after 20 years as their pastor, I retired in 2008.

One of the programs we decided to begin in the first few years was a <u>DIAL HOPE Telephone Outreach Ministry</u> that would be available 24 hours a day to help anyone in need of a spiritual lift. I recorded daily devotionals with a Scripture, a thought for the day, a prayer and an opportunity to request prayer. The devotionals were changed daily with a recorded sermon on Sundays.

We advertised DIAL HOPE, and our church program four times a year by sending out twelve thousand flyers, in the metropolitan newspaper, in our zip code areas and with a free ad in a countywide weekly newspaper. Over a sixteen year period we have had over fifty thousand calls with about five thousand requests for prayer.

It is my hope that some of the suggestions in this book will help pastors and churches, reach men and women who need the love and power of God to help them in their quest to lead lives of meaning, purpose, strength, peace and happiness beyond their dreams.

# Chapter One

## *Prayer Is the Key to Church, Renewal, Growth and Outreach*

The most important function for change in any church is prayer. Prayer is as powerful today as during Biblical times. Prayer is where everything begins and continues. Bathe everything in prayer. Jesus said "Ask and you shall receive," (Matthew 7:7). Jesus did not set limits on prayer requests.

Prayer is the basis of all church renewal, growth, and outreach. It is vital to a dynamic ministry. Bathe everything that happens in a church, in prayer.

Along with sermons based on the dynamics of a positive faith in God it is important to emphasize personal and corporate prayer that will help prepare and continue church renewal, growth, and outreach.

There are different kinds of prayers and all of them are valid at certain times and places. One of the most important forms of prayer for a church is Directed Silent Prayer. It involves everyone present, in the mission of the church in any service or meeting.

Silent prayer is a personal intimate expression of a person to God even for a person who may not usually pray. Directed silent prayer can be used in the following ways:

### Sunday Worship Services

During Sunday Worship Services, it is important to begin the prayer time with meditation and directed silent prayer. It is important to thank God for everything that He has done for us as individuals and as a church.

Then everyone prays silently for the congregational prayer requests as the names and requests are announced individually. (Individuals write the name and request on a prayer request form as they enter the church.) The pastor reads the name and the request. Everyone prays for that person and his or her request. Specific requests for God's guidance of the church should be included.

This is followed by a silent prayer time for personal confessions and personal prayer requests. Then included in the pastoral prayer that follows is a prayer of thanks that God is answering our prayers and a prayer for forgiveness of our sins followed by the regular pastoral prayer ending with the congregation praying the Lord's Prayer and the singing of a three fold "Amen." The Lord's Prayer and the singing of the "Amen" makes everyone part of the prayer experience and includes an outward corporate expression of the congregation.

This pattern of silent prayer, excluding the singing Amen, could begin every meeting of the church including the Deacons and Board meetings, men's and women's groups, Bible study groups, and of course the weekly prayer group.

### Weekly Prayer Group

A weekly prayer group is essential to the life of the church. Only a few people may attend, but it is powerful in the life of the pastor and the church program.

The time for a prayer group might be set for early Monday or Tuesday morning when the church office opens for business and may take about an hour. This starts the week with inspiration for everyone in the group.

When the Prayer Group meets, make a list of all the prayer requests from the Sunday Service and add other people and programs to it. Then have the pray list duplicated for each member.

Begin the meeting with a short Bible devotional or a short Bible video which will focus the group on God's will.

Then begin the prayer time with five minutes of non-directed silent prayer followed by directed silent prayers for individuals on the prayer list and others. Follow the silent prayers by sharing voluntary oral prayers with each other and with God. The pastor prays last and ends the prayer session with the Lord's Prayer.

The members take their prayer list copies with them for their daily prayer times and devotions.

### Prayer Chain

It is important to create a Prayer Chain that is activated for emergency prayer requests on a moment's notice. Each member of the Prayer Chain calls the next member with the request.

## *Personal Daily Prayer and Bible Reading*

A daily individual devotional time by the members and friends of the church helps keep the focus of the church on renewal, growth and outreach. Reading a page a day in the Psalms, Proverbs and the New Testament help individuals with the living of their lives and praying daily for the Sunday service prayer requests on the back page of the Sunday bulletins unites everyone on the church's mission to help people experience the presence of God.

As the Apostle Paul wrote in 1 Thessalonians 5:17, "Pray without ceasing. In everything, give thanks for this is the will of God in Christ Jesus for you," (NKJV).

God's guidance is the key to church renewal, growth, and outreach and prayer is the way to make it happen. When a pastor and all the members focus their thoughts and prayers asking for God's guidance, God will lead and guide them to do things that may seem impossible at the time.

*Never underestimate the power of God!*

# Chapter Two

## *Public Relations Begins with the Pastor and a Positive Faith in God*

Since the pastor is the key to a successful church renewal, growth, and outreach campaign, the pastor needs to lead the way with a strong positive, optimistic, enthusiastic faith that God will, lead and guide their church to grow and reach the unchurched with the Good News of the Gospel.

The pastor needs to accentuate the positive and never give anyone a guilt complex for not attending church, or not doing anything. My old preacher daddy used to say, *"If a person wants to do anything, they will find a way to do it, and if they don't want to do anything they won't do it, so don't give them an opportunity to use any of your negative remarks as a reason for not doing it."*

Negatives might go like this: *"I haven't seen you in church. You know you should attend more often"* or *"Where were you at the last family night? You missed a good program."* or *"You know you ought to attend the adult Bible class. It would be good for you."* How much better to say, *"I missed you at church."* Is anything wrong?

*Is there anything I can do to help?"* or *"We missed you at our last family night, hope you can come the next time."* or *"We're really having a good time learning and enjoying Christian fellowship in the adult Bible class. I know you'd enjoy it."*

I've never forgotten when I began my student pastorate in seminary, a nice elderly lady took me aside and said, *"Don't bawl us out for people who aren't here. It's not our fault that they aren't in church."*

In order to lead people, a pastor needs to have a strong positive, optimistic, enthusiastic faith in God that promotes the same attitude in the members.

The pastor needs to subtly begin a church renewal, growth, and outreach campaign because resistance is likely to happen. This is true when anything is proposed that requires change. It is necessary to slowly show and convince the members that church renewal, growth, and outreach has happened in other churches, and that it is possible in theirs.

This can be accomplished subtly with sermons based on the dynamics of a positive faith in God as recorded in the Bible using Hebrews 11, and other passages with modern day applications of how God continues to use dedicated people to reach today's unchurched people.

Some good illustrations of churches that help their members with renewal, growth and outreach projects are reported in current denominational magazines and will be presented in this book. It's important that the pastor share these illustrations as examples in sermons and get the members thinking about church renewal, growth, and outreach.

For many years a church was interested only in serving their own membership. They had built a group of friendly people that liked each other and they weren't interested in helping anyone else. A young girl began attending Sunday services on her own. They asked her about her parents and she told them they didn't want to attend church services but she wanted to attend and so she did. The church members decided to help the young girl by starting a Sunday School class for her. She liked it and began bringing friends to the class. The pastor and some of the members began to visit the parents of the children inviting them to church services. The members realized that the people next to the church needed the Lord and they began a renewal effort that continued to reach many more people for their church that caused it to grow and begin an outreach ministry. All because of one young girl finding God in her life.

Every church and every community situation is different in many ways. It is important to be flexible in creating a plan for renewal, growth and outreach.

# Chapter Three

## *Beginning the Process of Church Renewal, Growth, and Outreach Using God's Guidance and Public Relations Methods*

Back in the 1950's, a church only had to open its doors and people would flock to it. In today's world people have little interest in churches. For the past three decades every mainline denomination has lost members.

The church today needs to use modern methods to make the church appealing.

A major method of reaching people in today's world is through the use of public relations. Very few churches have included funds in their budgets for public relations, which can reach the unchurched in their community.

A definition of Public Relations for non-profit organizations, is to create a favorable acceptance of ideas, programs, and products of an organization to meet the needs of individuals, families, and the community. It is designed to bring about change and create action that will result in the active participation of people in an organization. A public relations person plans and creates special events and programs to promote a successful image of an occasion, whether or not, the event or program achieves its goal.

Public Relations uses all manners of techniques, including psychology, sociology, and advertising to persuade individuals to act and make changes in their lives.

Public Relations helps organizations grow and prosper.

In business organizations, any major public relations campaign begins with ideas. The key person to begin, motivate, and sell the campaign to the corporate board and the stockholders is the CEO. The CEO begins the process by presenting to the corporate board a "big picture" of ideas on how to increase sales by developing or improving products that will meet the needs, wants, and desires of the target customers. This in turn pleases the stockholders.

Public relations methods that change the public image and increase the bottom line, begin with the corporate board planning a public relations campaign and implementing the plan.

An outline of their plan of action is often to go back to basics; affirming the corporation's basic concepts, studying the product to find its present effectiveness, studying the target audience to determine how the product can be improved to appeal to more people, and creating a new image of the product and the corporation in the minds of the general public.

The same process is necessary to launch a major public relations church renewal, growth, and outreach campaign.

The key person to originate the ideas and begin, motivate, and sell the public relations campaign to the church board and the members is the CEO of the church, the pastor.

Using public relations methods, pastors and churches will be able to make it happen by beginning a church renewal process that includes raising the member's morale, providing attractive welcoming facilities, creating interesting and meaningful services with Bible study classes and programs that meet the needs of the members and friends of the church.

Then, by using public relations methods, a church can change the image of the church in the minds of the unchurched by developing outreach methods that touch everyone in the community and help create church growth.

# Chapter Four

## *The First Action of the Church Board Is to Plan a Public Relations Outreach Campaign*

Using sermons about faith and prayer and the power of God to guide individuals and churches will stimulate the thoughts of the members about their futures and the future of the church. Then the pastor/CEO needs to present his or her vision for church renewal, growth and outreach to the Church Board Members.

This can be accomplished by having the pastor call on some of the board members and share with them the ideas about possible ways church renewal, growth and outreach can be accomplished. The pastor should make sure to have several of the Board members agree with his or her ideas when they are presented. Once the board agrees with the ideas, they need to present them informally to the other church members.

The basic concept is to be a mission church and welcome everyone in the community to attend services and activities. The Board needs to discuss the three basic concepts needed for church renewal, growth and out-reach with a positive faith that God will work through the church to reach others in the community in spite of lim-ited resources.

The three basic concepts needed for church renewal, growth, and outreach is:

1. The church needs to state that it is a mission church and will accept anyone, regardless of their status in life.
2. A positive faith that God will work through their church to give the members hope and guidance.
3. The focus of every service and meeting needs to be on directed silent and expressed prayer for the church and others.

The board also needs to affirm that the church will trust God and will focus every service and every meeting on prayer, both silent and expressed, to ask for God's guidance and help.

# Chapter Five

## *Raising Church Morale and Hope for Church Renewal*

Based on the recent history of membership losses, many churches have low morale and a lack of hope for their future.

One of the best ways to unite all the members in a renewal, growth, and outreach campaign is to celebrate the past and the impact that their church has had on individuals and the community over the years.

Everyone needs to feel good about how their church has helped thousands of people in the past.

This will do two things: it will show the members how important their church has been in the past, and give them hope for how they can help people now, and in the future.

Every church has served their community and touched the lives of thousands of people through the years. Why not celebrate this wonderful legacy?

It is important to plan a "Heritage Weekend," and invite as many former pastors and members of the church as can be found to join in the celebration.

Begin by praying for the "Heritage Weekend" and asking for God's help.

Plan a specific weekend several months in advance. Plan for a potluck on a Saturday night, and then have the former pastors take part during the Sunday Worship Service the next day.

Begin by having the ladies compile names and addresses of former members, former pastors and surviving widows and widowers of former pastors. Have the ladies send invitations and make preparations to host the potluck.

Call the event "<u>A Walk Down Memory Lane</u>," with pictures and memorabilia placed in a special display the night of the potluck. Ask the former pastors and their wives to share some of their memories of the church, and how God has helped them with their ministries.

The excitement of the "Heritage Weekend" will build.

When the evening arrives, the former pastors, surviving former pastor's wives or husbands, and former members, will attend the celebration. The Church Hall will be filled with voices and laughter as old friends that haven't seen each other in years share what has been happening in their lives. The pastors will share their memories of the church and how God has guided their ministries after leaving the church. Individuals will add their anecdotes from the past and how God has blessed their lives.

It will be a real "homecoming" and it will bring inspiration and happiness to everyone. Pictures will be snapped and a video camera can record the entire celebration.

The Sunday Service will be packed with former members, and all the former pastors will participate. Everyone will feel God's presence and it will give everyone a feeling of hope.

What a glorious celebration! All the present members will begin feeling good about their church again.

From this "Heritage Weekend," the members will gain memories and experiences that they can use to remind them of how proud they should be when they think of how many people they have helped come to know God over the years.

As the pastor begins thinking about all the people who have been members of the church, he or she can search the membership records to see if any of them became pastors or leaders in the denomination over the years. This information would help the pastor to continue the theme of the "Heritage of The Church."

These former members could be honored with special weekends, which could be planned for each of those members who became pastors or leaders in the denominational church. On a Saturday night, they could be honored at a potluck "Roast," where their lives and accomplishments could be related. On Sunday they could be asked to preach and/or witness in the Worship Service. Plaques could be made for each of them with their photograph and a summary of their achievements. These could be placed at the entrance of the church sanctuary for everyone to see as they entered.

In this way, the church members can celebrate their heritage and continue to feel pride in their church. Their morale will rise, and the members will continue to have hope that their church can make a difference in the lives of the people in their community.

Every church has a glorious heritage that can be celebrated. It will unite the members and make God's power real in their church.

# Chapter Six

## *Planning and Resources for Church Renewal, Growth, and Outreach*

Once the members have celebrated their "Heritage Weekend" and have come to realize how important their church has been in so many lives, it is time to get them thinking about their church today, and what they can do to reach others for the Lord.

Every member needs to understand the church's circumstance and the need for renewal, growth, and outreach. This can be accomplished in many ways using the church newsletter, individual letters, congregational meetings, or individual calls by the Board members.

An excellent way to begin the process is to set up a church-wide planning conference to establish the needs of the congregation. The optimal time for this would be on a Saturday morning so that you could include as many members as possible.

Before the conference, develop a questionnaire listing all of the church services, programs and activities, and asking all of the members for their opinions, and suggestions for improvements to these programs that would help the church grow and reach others for the Lord. Include the questionnaires in the church newsletter with a response deadline before the planning conference.

Create an agenda for the conference based on the returned questionnaires. This will include input from all of the members including those who would not be able to attend.

Select a setting for the conference that would insure there would be no disturbances.

List all the suggestions from both the questionnaires, and those attending the conference, on a black board or some other visual aid. Lead a discussion about the suggestions and establish a prioritized list of projects to use as a guide.

A report of the results of the conference needs to be included in the church newsletter to keep all the members informed.

The Board needs to discuss the suggestions and priorities. It is important to get individual cost estimates for the projects, and decide which are possible within the current church budget. Some tasks require minimal financial resources, like designating a special Saturday to clean up the kitchen, pews, windows, and landscaping. A minor expense for some of the projects would be like paint, with a major requirement for volunteer painters.

If specific projects do not fall within the budget, it may be necessary to survey the members by having a Board member ask individuals or groups of individuals if they would like to donate the funds for a specific project. If they agree to sponsor a project, it will be important to honor them in some way. A church needed air conditioning. They asked a select group of members to fund it and they did. They were honored with a plaque placed in an appropriate place.

Another church had a large project: the re-stuccoing of the sanctuary building at an estimated cost of ten thousand dollars. This project would require a fund raising campaign. They prayed and asked for God's help. They began by presenting the need for the project in a congregational meeting, where they asked for the approval of the members. The members approved the project and reported it in the church newsletter, basing it on the congregational meeting's recommendation. They began the fund raising drive by using special offering envelopes in the church newsletter. The reason for using the church newsletter was that they often go to former members and friends that might contribute to the project. Then they waited to see what would happen.

To the surprise of everyone, the funds were raised without any other appeal. The members and friends of the church sent in their contributions. If people know the reason for a project they will respond.

The pastor and the members continued to bathe every action of the church in prayer and God supplied every need. The Apostle Paul writes to the Church of Philippi, "And my God will meet all your needs according to his glorious riches..." (Philippians 4:19 (NIV)) God will provide all our needs.

Every church's needs and resources are different. It's amazing what talents and resources the individuals in a church and in a community have to bring to any situation.

Once the members begin to feel the enthusiasm of their church's plans to grow and reach others with the Gospel, they will support the programs and projects. If the needs are beyond their resources, pray and keep praying. God will use many ways to provide the means.

God knows when a church does not have the financial resources to grow, and like Moses in the wilderness when God supplied all the needs of the people, God will supply its needs. Have faith that God will supply all the needs of a church and He will.

"Where there's a will there's a way" is true even today. Every situation is different and God will provide the resources if we keep a positive faith and pray to him for help.

*Never underestimate the power of God.*

# Chapter Seven

## *Attracting New People by Upgrading Facilities*

Every church wants to attract new people to their services and activities. Public relations suggests many ways to attract new visitors including the physical facilities of an organization.

A non-profit organization might have an outstanding program, but if the facilities are dirty or run down, a visitor may be "turned off" and never return.

I read somewhere that in order to attract new people, a church needs four things: attractive buildings; a good-looking sign since this is the first thing a person sees; clean, first-class restrooms are a must, especially for ladies; and a beautiful well run nursery for mothers of small children.

Many churches need to refurbish their facilities to welcome visitors. Too often the buildings and grounds have been neglected.

It is important to have all the members involved in refurbishing the facilities. A Men's Group, meeting once a month in a restaurant for breakfast, could set up monthly projects for the buildings, one Saturday a month. A Women's Group could meet monthly to plan projects for landscaping and refurbishing the furniture of the facilities.

Gradually, the refurbishing of the church takes place until all of the church facilities and grounds are ready to attract and welcome visitors and new members. The results of these projects will attract visitors to the church and then later perhaps the church membership.

# Chapter Eight

## *Creating Joyful, Meaningful Worship Services to Attract Visitors*

Any major public relations campaign in the business world needs a quality product that meets the needs of the established customers and attracts new ones. The corporate board needs to study the product to find its present effectiveness, study the target audience to determine how the product can be improved to appeal to more people, and create a new image of the product in the minds of the general public in order to improve the bottom line.

The same process needs to be applied to church services and programs.

Life is change! Nothing ever stays the same. It is important to recognize the changes that occur in life and make adjustments in order to supply answers for future changes. It is difficult to attract new people to a church that does not offer innovative services and programs.

To attract new people, it is important to have informal services with congregational participation that is personal and meaningful to the members and visitors alike.

Many members of any church have grown accustomed to their particular order of worship. It is important to respect their traditions and make changes only after careful consideration by the Board members. My old daddy, a pastor for 63 years, gave me some good advice when I became a pastor. He said, *"Son, don't change anything in a church until after you have laid a good foundation with the 'movers and shakers' of the church, and then move very carefully."*

All of the changes have to be made carefully and the reasons for the changes need to be shared with all the board members and the members to help the church grow. Change one thing at a time.

Often the Sunday Service's order of worship is traditional. I read somewhere that to attract younger people, it is important to have an informal service. It is also important to have congregational participation in the service. Develop a structured informal order of worship that is meaningful to members and visitors alike.

Some suggestions for moving toward a more structured informal order of worship are included in this chapter. These suggestions need to be evaluated by each pastor and the board and accepted or rejected based on the desires of the members.

If a church doesn't have a choir, the congregation can sing the responses which also involves them in the service. These responses can be choruses.

For modern responses, purchase a chorus book and begin singing choruses for the call to worship, before the prayer time, after the offering, before the sermon, and after the benediction. It seems like a lot of singing by the congregation but they will enjoy it. A man said, *"I'd rather have us singing the responses than a choir."* It is important to change the choruses about every three months. Use a denominational hymnal or chorus book for the choruses. These books have authorization from the original publishers for use with congregations. This avoids paying copyright fees every year.

Ten minutes before the service, a pastor could help members who are in need of personal prayers by sitting in front of the pews facing the congregation. Anyone desiring prayer can come to the front row pew. Then the pastor can take their hands, and ask for their specific prayer request and pray with them. As one lady said, "*It's wonderful to know that I can have the pastor pray with me, when I need it on any Sunday.*"

It is important to place an announcement in the Sunday bulletin stating that, "The pastor will pray with anyone who desires it before the service. Please come to a front row pew."

For a welcoming atmosphere, the organist can play a mini-concert on the piano or organ beginning fifteen minutes before the service. The mini-concert can include all kinds of music until the time for the prelude. Members will begin coming early to listen to the mini-concert.

It is necessary to define the end of the mini-concert and the beginning of the service. In appreciation of the concert, the organist can be thanked by the pastor with everyone clapping their approval.

Then everything can stop while a student lights the candles on the altar. This indicates the beginning of the worship service.

The service begins by singing a call to worship chorus. This is followed by a call to worship, and a prayer by the pastor.

In order to create a friendly atmosphere, after the singing of the first hymn, while everyone is standing, the pastor invites the people to shake hands with their neighbors. A suggested invitation might be:

*"The Christian Church is a Christian Fellowship. It is people loving and caring, and sharing joys and sorrows together. It is people reaching out to others. As an act of Christian Fellowship greet your neighbors at this time."*

Everyone greets each other by walking around the sanctuary before the service continues. It "breaks the ice," welcomes visitors, and helps the congregation to "bond" in worship.

To keep the focus on the mission of the church, the congregation could join in reading aloud an affirmation prayer printed in the bulletin. A suggested affirmation prayer might be:

*"We believe that God will lead us to be a strong spiritual influence for good in our community. We believe that God can, and will help us to reach others with the Good News of the Gospel. We believe that God can, and will heal and help those for whom we pray. Holy Spirit, come with power into our lives, and into our church. Show us what we can do to help others. In Jesus' Name, Amen".*

After singing a prayer chorus, a time of silent prayer could begin by the pastor suggesting everyone thank God for all the good things that have happened to them and are happening to the church.

This could be followed by Directed Silent Prayer by the pastor for all the personal congregational prayer requests, and needs of the church. The pastor reads the names and the requests from a prayer request list, which the congregation members fill out upon entering the church. These are brought to the pastor during the singing of the first hymn. As a request is read, everyone prays silently for that request.

A time for silent personal confessions and prayers follows making the prayer time personal for everyone.

The Pastoral Prayer needs to always include thanking God for answering our prayers, and asking for forgiveness of sins, followed by the Lord's Prayer and the singing of a threefold "Amen," by the congregation.

This same outline of prayer may be used before Bible classes, men's and women's groups, and Deacons and Board meetings without the "Amen." To make the pastoral prayers, calls to worship, and opening prayers meaningful to the congregation, a pastor may take any written prayer and rewrite it using conversational English, getting away from stilted words and phrases.

A pastor may use verses from the Psalms for the Calls to Worship, and create special prayers for special days of the year like Christmas, Easter, Mother's Day, etc. All Calls to Worship, Opening Prayers and Pastoral Prayers may be used over as needed.

The Prayer Time in the service can be followed by a solo or special musical number. The music can be altered from time to time with instrumental music by youth symphony orchestra members, a Christian Barber Shop Quartet, Sunday School children singing, or youth choirs from large nearby churches. (Pay for special music is important within the means of the church budget.)

A "Time of Fellowship" may follow the prayer time that includes a welcome to visitors, special thanks to individuals for flowers etc., and announcements.

Following the "Fellowship Time" the congregation may stand for the Doxology as the ushers come forward to receive the offering. After a prayer, the ushers take up the offering. Then they bring it to the front of the sanctuary to be placed on the altar or communion table. A chorus response sung by the congregation may complete the offering ritual.

A time for the "Child in All of Us," may follow as all the children in the congregation come to the front of the church. They sit facing the pastor who is sitting on a chair facing the congregation. This makes it their personal time with the pastor. The pastor then shares a story and may ask questions, and repeat the answers for the enjoyment of both the children and the congregation. The children's message needs to be light and short. A suggestion is to always end with the fact that no matter what happens in life, we can always find help from God. Ask the children how they can find God's help, with their responses being Sunday School, the Bible, prayer, and worship services. Close by having the children give the pastor "five" as they slap his or her hand.

The Scripture or Responsive Scripture Reading can follow, read by a layperson, giving the pastor a break before the sermon.

Following a chorus, before the sermon, the pastor begins the message of the morning. Good inspirational sermons are a must for a growing church. (There are many sermon help magazines on the market to help with sermon preparation.) It is important for the pastor to include a time in every sermon for everyone to make a decision to follow the Lord like concluding with: *"If we want God's help in our lives we need to dedicate or rededicate our lives to God in silent prayer."* Then suggest a simple prayer with, *"Just pray, Heavenly Father, come into my life. Forgive my sins and help me. In Jesus' Name, Amen."* After a few moments of silent prayer, the pastor ends the sermon with a short prayer. (As an outreach act, it is important to challenge people all the time with a decision to follow the Lord.)

The service ends with a closing hymn, the Benediction and a closing chorus as the pastor walks to the entrance of the church to greet the people.

In order to create interest in the Sunday Services, a different subject might be part of every service on a continuing basis.

The first Sunday of the month might be a celebration of Holy Communion according to the doctrine of your church. The following order of worship for communion is just a suggestion if it falls within your church's tradition.

The order of worship of a Sunday service as suggested remains the same as other services through the sermon, which is followed by an invitation for everyone to partake of the elements. During the singing of the Communion Hymn, the elders or deacons come forward and sit in chairs near the Communion Table facing the congregation. The pastor sits behind the Communion Table and begins the service by reading I John 1:8, followed by everyone joining together in praying a printed unison prayer of confession from the bulletin, followed by reading I John 1:9. Then the pastor reads the institution of the Lord's Supper Scripture, (1 Corinthians 11:23-25) followed by a prayer of dedication. Those chosen to serve the elements, serve the bread to the pastor, the organist, choir and the congregation. Everyone holds the elements and the servers return to their chairs in the front of the sanctuary. The pastor serves the deacons or elders and then everyone partakes together. This is followed with the grape juice, a closing prayer, the congregational singing of the Lord's Prayer, and the Benediction.

The second Sunday of the month might have a favorite hymn sung after the Christian greeting time. Sing only the first verse of hymns called out by individuals, for about fifteen minutes. Everyone enjoys singing favorite hymns.

The third Sunday, have a lay person present a Minute for Missions, again after the Christian greeting time. This keeps the congregation informed about missions around the world.

The fourth Sunday, after the Christian greeting time, offer a time for prayer and healing for those who desire it for themselves or someone else. Those desiring prayer are asked to sit on the front row pew. The Elders or Deacons are asked to come to the front of the sanctuary. Then individually each person requesting prayer is asked to kneel or sit in a chair facing the front of the sanctuary. The Board members stand behind the person. They place their hands on the person's shoulders. The pastor places his hands on the head of a person kneeling or takes the hands of the person seated requesting prayer. Then he or she asks the person their name and their request. The pastor then asks the congregation to pray silently for the person's request. The pastor prays aloud for the request. This can be a real blessing for everyone.

### Benedictions

For variety, a pastor may choose use any of these suggested Benedictions that I used for 20 years. Put them in the back of a Book of Common Worship.

May the glory of the Lord fill your hearts and minds, and guide you in everything that you do. For God will keep your life, and in him you will have a home forever. Amen.

Jesus said, "Peace be with you. As the Father sent me, even so, I send you." Let us go forth from this hour remembering that whatever we do, in word or in deed, we do in the name of our Lord Jesus Christ. Amen.

May the God of peace fill your lives with the power of the Holy Spirit, and keep you safe from all harm. Hold on to what is good, and let the Spirit increase within you. Be joyful in your life, and in all things give thanks to God. For he has called you to a life of faith, and he will not fail you. Amen.

Out of the infinite glory of God the Father almighty, let Christ dwell within your hearts through faith, and let the power of the Holy Spirit keep you rooted and grounded in love, so that you will be filled with the fullness of God now and always. Amen.

May the word of God abide in your heart and soul, as you go forth to make disciples among all peoples, remembering the promise of Christ: "I am with you always, even to the end of time." Amen.

May the Lord be generous in increasing your love for one another and for the whole human family, as much as he has loved you. May you continue to strive toward the life which we are called to live, and God will confirm your hearts in holiness. Amen.

May the Gospel of our Lord Jesus Christ come upon you not only through words, but as the power of the Holy Spirit working within you. Receive his truth with confidence and assurance, knowing that through faith, hope, and love, you will accomplish God's work in the world. Amen.

Dedicate your life to the Lord, and you will belong to his kingdom and dwell secure. Have hope in him; hold firm in your faith, take heart. Yea, hope in the Lord! Go now in peace. Remember that God loves you. And in all that you do, serve him and one another. Amen.

Jesus said, "As the Father has loved me, I have loved you. Remain in my love so that my joy may dwell within you, and your joy will be complete." Amen.

It is important to make every informal service a joyful celebration, and based on Psalm 150, applaud after the piano mini-concert, the special music, and when appropriate during the announcements. The members will enjoy participating in the service. Some people will always prefer a more formal worship service, but gradually they will accept the modifications in order to attract the younger people. Each church must determine their own worship needs and desires, but in order to attract younger visitors it may require some compromises. These ideas are just suggestions. They may or may not appeal to some churches.

During special Sundays like Mother's Day and Father's Day, three or four lay persons can read poems or share their thoughts and memories as part of the service to make the day special and personal.

On other Sundays throughout the year, have a Chancel Drama Group, composed of some of the members, put on short Christian reader's theater productions with the members reading from scripts. The scripts can be purchased through Christian book stores.

On Christmas Eve, the Chancel Drama Group can make the birth of Jesus real by putting on a short play, from a different viewpoint each year, followed by the traditional candlelight service.

During Holy Week, for small churches, have a combined Maundy Thursday-Good Friday Service on Thursday evening. This service begins with the observance of the Lord's Last Supper with his disciples and includes the Seven Last Words from the cross.

Easter is a joyous celebration. A suggestion to make it different and special, might be an Easter Canary Service with canaries singing throughout the service. About a month before Easter, contact a bird pet store and tell the manager that you are planning for an Easter Canary Service. Tell the manager that his or her store will be publicized extensively in the church newsletter, Easter flyers, and bulletins. Ask to borrow two singing canaries in separate cages on Friday and return them on Monday. (When you put two canaries in one cage they will not sing, but will fight for dominance.) About three weeks before Easter, ask the person who feeds the canaries to watch the canaries and select two singing canaries for Easter.

Put the canaries in the balcony so they will not be distracted by the audience, and take away their food during the service or they may just eat. (To guarantee singing canaries, have a back up tape recording of canaries singing that can be purchased at the pet store. Have a person sit in the balcony to turn the tape recording on if necessary.) Most of the time, the tape recording will not be needed. It makes a glorious Easter Service that will be remembered by everyone in attendance. (Putting a flyer in the newspaper, promoting the Canary Easter Service, will cause many of the unchurched to attend the service out of curiosity.)

These ideas may help create informal services with congregational participation that will be joyful, personal, and meaningful.

# Chapter Nine

## *Beginning or Stimulating a Sunday School*

Children need all the help they can get in today's world with the problems of divorce, drugs, alcohol and temptations from the movies, television, and the internet.

It is very easy for children who face peer pressure to experiment with things that may cause disastrous results in their lives.

It is important for every church, even small ones that may not have had a Sunday School in recent years, to make Sunday or Church School classes as interesting, exciting, and meaningful as possible, to instill values in the children that will help them make the right choices in life.

For Churches that have Sunday Schools, this chapter may have some ideas that could help your Sunday School, but it is written primarily to help churches that do not have a Sunday School and want to begin one.

Small churches without a Sunday School face a dilemma: they want younger families with children to attend their church for growth and outreach, but they do not have Sunday School classes for the children. It isn't easy to begin a Sunday School when there are no school-aged children in the member families.

Some people think that having a tiny Sunday School is not worth the effort. I read about one of these small churches that had only one little girl who regularly came to their church all alone. After some soul searching, the members decided that they should provide a Sunday School class for that little girl, and they did it. The little girl grew up to be an outstanding leader in their church and their denomination. It is important to have even a tiny Sunday School to help even one little girl.

Begin planning for a Sunday School, by making it a matter of prayer. Seek God's guidance at every worship service, every meeting, and in every individual's daily devotions.

About six months before the Fall Semester of the school year, set up several committees to plan and co-ordinate the beginning of a Sunday School.

The needed committees include: The Curriculum Committee, The Facilities and Equipment Committee, The Volunteer Teacher Committee, a Public Relations Committee, and a Central Committee. In a small church two or three people can be a committee.

A Central Committee composed of the leaders of each of the planning committees will meet periodically to coordinate the work of the committees.

The Curriculum Committee should include the pastor and any members that are, or have been, school teachers. The pastor needs to secure several sample Sunday School Curricula for nursery through high school classes and if there is no adult class, materials or video/DVD courses that could be used to create one.

The curriculum needs to be studied by the pastor for theological emphasis that corresponds to the church members' beliefs.

The teachers need to study the needs and focus on which materials would be easy for teachers to prepare and that would interest the different age groups. Since teachers have a limited amount of time to prepare, it is important to make their preparation as easy as possible.

To make Sunday School exciting for the children, the Curriculum Committee needs to plan for, and select Bible centered cartoon videos/DVDs that can be included in the beginning assembly of the children, along with the singing of choruses. (How to secure the equipment, and use it with the adult classes will be included in chapter 11.) The regular teacher's lesson will follow. There should be a time for snacks, since children get hungry.

To make the teenage students' class interesting and exciting, in addition to regular Sunday School materials, Christian videos/DVDs can help them learn Christian values and answer teen problems.

It is not necessary to purchase all of the videos/DVDs until the time to begin the class draws near, but it is important to have a few of the children's cartoon Bible videos/DVDs for the first few sessions.

When the pastor and teachers have selected a curriculum, and the cartoon and teen videos/DVDs that meet the requirements of that curriculum, the committee will recommend their findings to the Central Committee.

The Facilities and Equipment Committee made up of the pastor and volunteer men will find, clean up and paint the classrooms. They need to recommend securing any necessary equipment for teaching like black boards etc. and report their plans to the Central Committee.

The Volunteer Teacher Committee's main purpose is to find volunteer teachers for the Nursery, Beginners, Juniors, Junior High, High School, and Adult classes. Even though there may not be students for all the classes, it is necessary to have teachers ready and prepared for all age groups, for the first two or three weeks. The sample curriculum materials can be used for the first few Sundays, and then more materials can be ordered.

The pastor needs to find teacher training materials, and then coordinate with a retired school teacher to set up convenient times for the volunteer teachers to meet for training before the Sunday School begins.

The leader of the committee needs to report their plans to the Central Committee.

A Public Relations Committee is responsible for publicizing the important message that the church is beginning something new to the target audience.

The P.R.Committee should be composed of the pastor, and anyone working with the media. The Committee needs to begin working on a time line for public relations activities leading up to the beginning of the Sunday School.

In order to create enthusiasm for the Sunday School in the members and friends of the church, the committees' progress reports need to be included in the Church Newsletter every month, from the planning stage, all the way through, to the beginning of the classes.

It is important to plan a major event that will focus the church members and the community on the beginning of the Sunday School.

A "Bring a Friend Sunday" could be the major publicity event to begin the Sunday School. This will include several months of planning and preparation.

Eight to ten weeks before the event, the pastor needs to invite his or her, "<u>Celebrity Friends</u>," to attend the Sunday Service and say a few words of greeting. This could include the Mayor or a City Council Member or a local TV News Anchor or someone connected to sports. The pastor can "sell" the "Celebrity Friends" on attending the service by letting them know that their photographs will be featured on the ten thousand to fifteen thousand flyers that will be distributed with the newspapers in the church's area. Celebrities like publicity and they will welcome the exposure.

Depending on the situation, guest musicians such as a harpist or a flautist may be invited and paid to provide special music for the service.

Every member needs to pledge, at least four weeks in advance and in writing, that they will bring visitors with them to this Sunday Service. This can be done using the Sunday bulletin. The members can invite these guests by giving them a flyer and telling them who the celebrity guests will be.

The flyers need to include not only the photos of the "Celebrity Friends" but should promote the Bible-centered cartoon videos/DVDs and what each age group will be studying and any other new activities in the church.

Before making the invitations and creating the flyers, the pastor needs to contact a newspaper editor to find out how many flyers will be needed and the distribution cost. The cost of printing or copying the flyers is necessary to determine the total cost of the project. In small towns, the editor may help the pastor with feature stories and low cost ads.

The Church Board needs to be briefed on the project and approve the action and the necessary finances.

If it is possible, have the members call on some families with children in their neighborhood. Tell them about the new Sunday School, and ask if they would like to attend with their children or if they would like them to take the children to Sunday School. Give them a flyer about "Bring-a-Friend Sunday," and invite the family to meet the member for the service at the church on that Sunday.

The "Bring-a-Friend Sunday" will be the public relations event that will bring parents and children to the church.

The Sunday before the "Bring-a-Friend Sunday," dedicate the teachers to God and to their Sunday School classes during the Sunday Service.

When the "Bring-a-Friend Sunday" arrives, there will be children and younger families. It may be only a small Sunday School, but at least there will be some younger families and children in the Sunday Service. Include special bulletins for the children that can be copied and handed out at the Sunday Worship Services. Also add a special time for the children to be with the pastor during the service.

For special occasions, the children can learn choruses or take part in a children's bell choir of eight bells that are color coded with an adult flashing color cards to create the music. (These bells are nothing like the adult bell choirs. They are inexpensive.)

In the future, on Wednesdays when the children get out of school early, a volunteer can hold a children's Christian fun time with crafts, games, stories and snacks. The children will love it and it will help the parents by giving the children an activity after school under supervision.

It is not easy to start a Sunday School from scratch, but it can be done.

# Chapter Ten

## *Junior Memberships and Church Scholarships Keep Children and Youth Interested in the Church*

One of the most difficult problems in churches today is to keep Jr. High and High School youths interested, and participating in a church.

Think about it. Major and minor league baseball and football teams all have Junior Member Clubs that give boys and girls recognition and status with special times for them to meet the players and get pamphlets and pictures.

Why not offer Junior Memberships in a church for boys and girls that will give them special recognition? This would be a way of helping junior boys and girls feel welcome and part of their church. Then when they become teenagers, they can become Adult Members and take active roles in the church by teaching children in the Sunday School and by taking on other church responsibilities. This will help them continue to be active in the church.

It happened in our church quite by accident. After we began our Sunday School before the service, children began attending Sunday Services that included a children's bulletin and a time with the pastor. A lady came to me and apologized for her granddaughter because she always marked "Church Member" when she signed her name on the Friendship Pad during the Sunday Service.

An idea for Junior Membership hit me! Why not have Junior Members in our church?

I proposed the creation of Junior Memberships in our church to the Church Board as a way of helping junior boys and girls feel welcome and part of the church. They agreed, and we set up the requirements to become a Junior Member. They included:

1. A child must be in third grade or older.
2. A child must complete a <u>Basic Christian Beliefs Course</u> that includes discussions at their level of understanding about God, Jesus Christ, the Holy Spirit, the Bible, The Christian Church, Communion, Baptism, Worshipping God, Prayer, Rules for Living, and becoming a Church Member. (A suggested Junior Members Basic Christian Beliefs Course is included in the appendix of this book.)
3. A child must be baptized either as an infant or by their choice.
4. The child will be officially welcomed during a Sunday Service by the pastor and elders.
5. A Junior Member will not be able to vote until they become an adult member of the church.
6. Junior Members will be given opportunities to

serve as acolytes and in other activities.

When the child is old enough to become an adult member of the church, he or she will attend a confirmation or church membership course and be welcomed as an adult voting member of the church.

We found that many of our Sunday School juniors had not been baptized. For six weeks, I taught a "Basic Christian Beliefs Course" on Wednesday afternoons when the juniors got out of school early. When they completed the course, and they dedicated their lives to the Lord, we baptized them and made them Junior Members of our church giving them certificates and lapel pins. They were really proud of becoming Junior Members of the church.

We had a class for two teen students. To make their class interesting and exciting, we relied on regular Sunday School materials and videos that focused on teen problems. The teens enjoyed the class and they learned Christian values. They became church members and both of them went on to college and received our church scholarships. Both of them became Deacons in our church.

Our Sunday School continued ten years after it began, and we had younger families and children in our church as we had planned.

(Note: to those churches planning to begin a Sunday School, read Chapter Nine.)

### *A Scholarship Fund*

It is important that young people continue to be active in the church and that they become the leaders of the church in the future. One way that this can be accomplished is to help them, even in a small way, as they prepare for their future life.

Our church received two gifts totaling fifteen thousand dollars. The Board voted to bank the money and establish a Scholarship Fund to help students active in our church services and activities based on the annual interest of the fund. This insures that it will be a perpetual fund.

It was decided that students who wanted to apply for a scholarship would be required to be active in the Church and write a paper of approximately five hundred words on the subject, "What God and the Church Mean to Me." They are to be employed having a part time or full time job or have extenuating circumstances of need. The applications would be reviewed by a Scholarship Committee and recommendations would be submitted to the Church Board. The Board selects the recipients. These scholarships may be limited to one or two hundred dollars annually in order to include as many students as possible. The honor of being selected helps the student in many ways.

The Scholarship Fund is open ended and welcomes contributions from anyone wishing to honor relatives, friends or contributors with their names permanently inscribed on a plaque and placed at the entrance of the sanctuary. As the Fund grows more scholarships will be added or the amounts of the awards will be increased.

The Church Board felt that having a job shows a serious determination by the student to acquire an education.

This is a good public relations program since these students will promote their church to other students and the parents and members will be proud of their church for helping the students.

# Chapter Eleven

## *Making Adult Classes Exciting and Meaningful*

People today want interesting, factual, graphic presentations, taught by experts in all areas of life. This is also true in teaching adult Bible classes.

Leadership for teaching Bible classes in most churches is at a premium. To help teachers prepare and teach their classes with a minimum of preparation, the teachers will welcome audio or video/DVD courses.

Using audio tapes, the expert teaches the teacher the lesson at home. The teacher takes notes and then uses the notes to teach the course.

Using video/DVD courses, the teacher reads the introductory material that comes with each class session, introduces the video/DVD, shows the video/DVD, and then leads a discussion about the video/DVD presentation during the class period.

All of the audio and video/DVD courses include materials that can be copied and given to the students at each session.

Buy inexpensive three ring notebooks for each student. Punch three holes in the copies and give them to the students for their notebooks.

Students like to receive the notes each week. Then they can study the material at home during the week. An important suggestion is to look for videos/DVDs that are filmed on the location of the original teachings in the Bible or illustrate the teachings with other visual information. Nothing is more boring than viewing a "talking head" with a professor teaching from a classroom environment.

Often the audio courses are produced with professional notes that can be purchased inexpensively for each student. These notes are used during the class, which helps the students understand the lesson.

For video/DVD courses, secure a secondhand color television set from a thrift store, and a new inexpensive VCR/DVD player. Put the TV and the VCR/DVD player on a movable stand with wheels like school equipment that can be purchased at a slightly used office supply store. Then the TV can be moved to different classrooms and it can be secured during the week in a locked room.

Similar TV sets can be obtained for the children's Sunday School Bible stories and for youth groups.

Another use for the TV/DVD video sets can be for an outreach ministry to offer classes for the people of the community. There are excellent video/DVD courses taught by experts on Marriage Enrichment, Parenting, Single Parenting, Divorce Recovery, Coping with Grief, and Setting Boundaries. The courses are taught by Christian psychologists, teachers, and pastors and will enrich the lives of individuals who attend them. These courses can be offered during the Sunday School hour and their children can attend Sunday School at the same time or they can be offered during the week.

It is possible to offer courses taught by a volunteer professional like a Christian psychologist leading a "<u>Divorce Recovery Course</u>" or perhaps a retired nurse leading a "<u>Coping with Grief Workshop</u>." They might use a video/DVD course as a basis for their class.

Some people have expressed their appreciation for these types of courses.

An engaged couple wrote:

*"We found the <u>Marriage Enrichment Course</u> an invaluable source of information. We learned a lot of helpful hints for a successful marriage. We developed our own personal goals and self desires. We would recommend this course to both married and premarital couples."*

From a recent divorcee:

*"I took a six week course on '<u>Divorce Recovery</u>.' I had been a member of the church for about a year and was struggling with life after our divorce. I found the course very helpful because it brought to light a lot of questions I had on how other people handle situations, child rearing, and standards for rebuilding a new life."*

From a single parent:

*"Being a single parent, I found the '<u>Single Parent Parenting Course</u>' very beneficial. They were very instructive. I found them to be comforting in the sense, that they helped me to understand that I'm not alone in my problems as a single parent. They seemed to instill the*

*spiritual confidence I needed to be a successful single parent. Thank you and God Bless."*

The modern video/DVD courses help the teachers and the students with their understanding of the Scriptures and how they can apply the Bible teachings to their every day lives. These courses also help people with other problems in life.

# Chapter Twelve

## *Improving a Church's Image Using Public Relations Methods*

From my ten years experience as a professional Public Relations Director, I realize that it's important to create a good public image of the church to attract visitors and new members from the community.

### *Important Factors to Attract Visitors*

Attractive facilities and grounds say to everyone, *"Welcome to Our Church."* I read somewhere that there are four things visitors look for in a church: well-kept buildings, an attractive sign, clean and modern restrooms, and a beautiful, well staffed nursery for preschool children. (See Chapter Seven for details on these suggestions.)

### *Saving Money with Memorable Sunday Bulletin Covers*

Positive first impressions for visitors attending Sunday Services include a warm welcome by the greeters and an attractive Sunday bulletin. Commercial bulletin covers are colorful, but to lower the cost and make bulletin covers that enhance the church's image, take a black and white photograph of the front of the church without cars or people (see the next section for taking black and white photographs.) Create your own bulletin cover using a computer and having it professionally printed on different colored paper. Not only will it reduce the cost of bulletin covers but it will give the visitors a visual image of your church to take home with them.

## Creating Church Newsletters That Promote Church Programs and Activities

Church newsletters can be an evangelism tool that creates a positive image of a church's programs for members, friends and visitors.

They say *"one picture is worth a thousand words."* Nothing can create more interest or enthusiasm in a church than photographs of church activities.

For eighteen years, I took black and white photographs using a 35mm camera and black and white print film for church activities, since copy machines cannot print photographs from color prints. It required buying black and white film, having it developed and printed by special photo labs, since photo shops developed and printed only color film. It was a hassle.

Then digital cameras became popular as they processed both color and black and white film in every photo shop. It made taking color and black and white prints possible from the same photograph. It also meant you could select and print only the photos you wanted to use in your newsletter and you didn't need to develop a whole roll of film for only three or four photographs.

Digital cameras are a little complicated to learn to operate, but every camera store will assist you and many of them offer free monthly evening classes of how to use digital cameras.

After using the digital camera for a few months, and after some advanced classes, you may learn to print your own photographs on your home computer.

In the meantime, you can take your camera and film to a photography shop, and they will give you a proof sheet with small photos of all the pictures on your film. Then you select the photos you want printed in either black and white, or color. They will make copies of the photos in the size you desire for your newsletter.

It is necessary to purchase a digital camera with six or more megapixels in order to make prints with the details you desire.

Using a digital camera, take two or three photos of each subject and view the photos to be sure you have the photo you want for your newsletter. The photo store can make glossy black and white print photographs to the size you need for the newsletter. Then stick the photos and their captions on the original newsletter copy with rubber cement.

To create a newsletter with photographs take an 8½ x11 piece of paper and make two columns. The column on the left will have the photographs and the right column will have the copy.

Make a first page "shell" consisting of the newsletter heading that can be used every month. Attach the shell to a piece of cardboard to make it permanent. The new photos and copy can be taped below the heading each month.

Put the pastor's thoughts on the back of the first page.

The third page will continue articles from page one with photographs on the left and copy on the right.

The rest of the pages, without photographs, will be full page text.

The last page, a mailing page, needs to be set up so that the newsletter can be folded in half to create two sides: the mailing side for the address and the other side to advertise the church programs and activities.

The mailing side should have a small map of where the church is located, while the other side should have the title, "Inside This Issue," and should list the highlights of the new programs. In a column on the right side it should also list the ways in which the church is serving the community by providing rooms for activities like Alcoholic Anonymous or Gamblers Anonymous Meetings, Boy Scouts, Girl Scouts etc. It should also list days and times for these meetings.

The mailing side will be the same for every issue. Only the "Inside This Issue" side will change. When getting the newsletter ready for mailing, use a piece of scotch tape to seal the folded newsletter. Never use staples. Make it as easy as possible for people to open the newsletter.

When you take the original newsletter to be copied at a copy center, ask them to be careful in printing the photos. Most copy centers have machines that read the difference in each page and make the adjustments needed. These machines print clear photos, collate the pages and staple the newsletters.

When writing copy for the newsletter always be positive and upbeat. Make sure that details are given for each activity. Attract the attention of the reader with the first line of the news item. Advertisers say that if you don't grab the reader's attention in the first eight seconds, forget it. An example might be, "<u>WANT TO IMPROVE YOUR MARRIAGE</u>?" or "<u>CREATE A HAPPY MARRIAGE</u>!" A Marriage Enrichment Video/DVD Course begins...etc." Not just "A Marriage Enrichment Video/DVD Course begins etc." Read all the copy and ask yourself, *"If I were a stranger would I be interested in this activity?"* If not, rewrite it.

The focus of the first page should be on new and future programs and events that would be interesting to members and visitors alike. This emphasis should continue for every new program or activity. It is important to plan and time your newsletter around new programs or activities that will capture the interest of the members and visitors. Distribute the newsletter the Sunday before the new program begins.

If there are no new planned programs or activities for a month, promote an existing program by reporting something interesting about it. For example in January report the inspiration of the Christmas activities with photographs. People like to read about events they have witnessed. It can stimulate those who didn't attend to think about attending the next time. Newspaper sports writers do this all the time.

A good place for the pastor's thoughts is page two. The pastor's thoughts section should always be positive and interesting. Nothing turns people off more than reading something negative about the church, or the budget, or a program. Keep the pastor's comments upbeat and positive with plenty of "<u>Kudos</u>" for individuals or groups. Always end with a friendly comment like *"See You in Church."*

Page three should continue programs from page one

with photographs on the left side of the page and copy on the right side of the page.

The remaining pages may be filled with Board notes, recognitions for services rendered, members' travels, birthdays and calendar activities.

In addition to the members and friends of the church, mail newsletters to all visitors who attend over several months. One young lady that attended services a few times, dropped out. Several months later she came back to the services. She said, *"Thanks for not giving up on me."* She later taught a Sunday School Class, led a mid-week children's activity program and led a Daily Vocation Bible School Class.

### Flyers That Reach the Unchurched

Flyers in local newspapers are an excellent way to reach the unchurched in your area. It will give them news of the programs and activities of the church. If you have a local newspaper in your area, inquire about the cost of placing a one page flyer in the newspaper. If you do not have a local newspaper, most metropolitan newspapers will quote prices for zip code areas. Then you can have the flyers printed or the newspaper may print them for you, depending on the cost.

To attract the attention of the reader, have the flyers printed on colored paper. Stay with light colors and black ink. Yellow attracts more attention than other colors and black ink is the most inexpensive.

When creating the original flyer with a computer, always create a "Hook" in the headline. A "Hook" headline is something that will grab the attention of the readers and give them a reason to continue reading the flyer. A

"Hook" headline might be "IT ISN'T EASY RAISING CHILDREN TODAY!" Then begin the first line with "A Free Parenting Video/DVD Course, taught by experts begins… etc." Use a "Hook" headline instead of a church heading on the flyer. Put the church heading and information at the bottom of the flyer and include a small photograph of the church and a small map of where it is located along with the address and phone number for information. If you use the church heading at the top of the flyer, the unchurched will see that it is from the church and toss it without reading it.

Follow your lead story with any new or special church programs beginning the Sunday following the distribution of the flyers in the newspaper. Use black border boxes around an announcement to attract attention.

Don't expect an immediate overwhelming response to the flyers. Direct mail companies hope for a three to five percent return and religion is a harder sell than a commercial item. One way to look at it is that everyone in the community becomes familiar with the church programs and if the church gets only a few new members from the flyers over the years they will have paid for the flyer.

Questions from pastors of other churches that see the flyers are often about the cost versus the results. Flyers have many positive effects on the church members. Their self-esteem grows as they discover that others know about the church programs, and that they are reaching the unchurched in the area. They also feel comfortable about inviting others to come to their church. Another positive effect is on the other pastors and churches of the same denomination in the local area. The results are more than just the cost of the flyers.

Publish flyers about four times a year but always

promote at least one new program. Direct mail advocates know that to be successful, a prospective customer has to receive their flyer at least three times before they will act. It may take several flyers to see results. Remember flyers are like digging in a gold mine. You may not hit gold for many days, but eventually you will. That's the way it is with the flyers.

With the cost of mailing everything going up, direct mail seems to be too expensive and complicated for sending flyers through the mail at this time.

# Chapter Thirteen

## *Promoting a Church's Image Using Newspapers, Magazines, Radio, Television and the Internet*

From a year of graduate study in public relations and ten years experience as a professional Public Relations Director, I'd like to share some Public Relations techniques that can promote a church's image.

Journalism reports what has happened; Public Relations makes it happen.

Public Relations is not always what happens, but what seems to have happened. A photograph of a few people at an event may be thought of by those who read about it as a big successful event when it was only a small group of people at a small event.

Public Relations is a strategy to favorably influence a target audience in reference to a specific organization, institution or individual by creating special events and happenings.

It is important to decide who your audience really is and plan a typical yearly calendar of public relations events.

The following suggestions come from the experience of a small church and can be modified for larger churches.

## *A Suggested Calendar for Public Relation Happenings during the Church Year*

The church public relations calendar includes some annual celebrations like Christmas and Easter, but it is also important to plan special events for every month of the church year.

Some suggestions for a church calendar might include:

December - Advent with special programs for each Sunday, such as inviting a bell choir from a nearby church to play during a Sunday Service before they play for their church or inviting a junior or youth choir from another church before they sing for their church or finding an instrumental group to play one Sunday.

You may also have your own children put on a modified Christmas pageant one Sunday even if you don't have enough children for all the parts. With a tiny Sunday School, have one Shepherd, one wise man, one angel, a Mary and a Joseph, and an older child to read the Scripture. If a member of the cast gets sick use a volunteer adult. The message is important for the Sunday School children and the worshippers.

On Christmas Eve, plan for the Chancel Drama Group (volunteer adults) to do a reader's play about the nativity and have an instrumentalist like a flute player and a soloist present favorite Christmas music.

A church can share their Christmas with seniors in a senior's complex on a Sunday afternoon by singing carols with them and putting on a Christmas Party. Often the manager of the complex already has a Christmas Party planned. If so, then invite the members of the church to sing Christmas Carols with them and enjoy the fellowship.

Publicize the Christmas Events and any future events by taking black and white photographs of anyone who will participate. If a bell choir will come one Sunday, take a photo when they are rehearsing in November and put the picture in the December newsletter. If you have a community newspaper give them a black and white glossy print and a news release about two weeks before the event. Small newspaper editors welcome black and white glossy prints and articles.

January - In the January church newsletter include photos that were taken during Christmas and write about the joy of the Christmas Celebration. You might begin a new class on Parenting or Marriage Enrichment on Sunday mornings during the Sunday School hour. (Children can attend Sunday School at the same time.) Send a news release to a newspaper. Send photos with the news release to a local newspaper. They also like presentations of awards or shows of appreciation especially for individuals in their publication area. They like publicity photos of people or events that will be happening in the future.

January or February is a good time to feature a heritage weekend and celebrate the past in some way with a potluck and by inviting a former pastor to bring the message on a Sunday.

February – You can feature Boy Scout and Girl Scout Sundays. The children from the Sunday School can sing during a Sunday Service.

Lent happens during March and April with special events leading up to Easter. During Holy Week plan for a high school trumpeter to play on Palm Sunday. For small churches on

Maundy Thursday Evening combine Holy Communion with Good Friday and have the Chancel Drama Group put on a short reader's drama or a reading about Good Friday such as "The Seven Last Words." A sermon isn't necessary. On Easter, have a glorious service using canaries and special music as described in Chapter Eight.

May is Mother's Day and in some areas Graduation Day. Use mothers and graduates in a service.

June is Father's Day, Children's Day, Graduations and Weddings. Do something special with one or more of these subjects.

July and August - Feature the Daily Vacation Bible School. This is a good time to preach a series of sermons on the prophets or little known Books of the Old Testament or the Parables of Jesus. In the church newsletter feature photographs of guest pastors who will be leading the worship services during the pastor's vacation.

September and October - Plan for new video/DVD classes on Parenting etc., to coincide with the Sunday School Rally Day. Combine everything with "Bring a Friend to Church Sunday" which is detailed in Chapter Nine.

November - Plan for Advent and Christmas and celebrate Thanksgiving with a Harvest Potluck Dinner.

These are only suggestions to help focus on specific interest areas and events. Some churches already have traditional activities that can be incorporated in the Public Relations Calendar.

### *Writing News Releases and Articles for Newspapers*

News releases or articles need to be interesting in order to "turn the editor on." Your headline has to sell. Begin with the most interesting sentence you can think of to stimulate the interest of the editor. Type it in all uppercase letters and present it as the title of your news release. Don't worry about the number of words. The editor will make his own headline. It has to attract the editor's attention. The editor is the only person you need to interest in your news release to get it published. Remember the word "News." Always include the "Who, What, When, Where, and Why." Put all of these facts in the first paragraph.

Create an eye catching title by asking a question like "Want to improve your marriage?" or by stating an unusual happening like "Enjoy a Joyous Canary Easter Service with Us." As I was taught when I sold insurance, "Sell the sizzle not the steak." The first sentence of an article has to grab the attention of the editor, since all editors get more articles than they can publish. Write and rewrite your news release. Read it aloud and rewrite it until you feel that a stranger would find it interesting. Use sentences like, "The men will be meeting for breakfast," instead of "The men will meet for breakfast" to stimulate interest. Using "ing" words brightens any copy, and makes it more appealing in bulletin announcements, newsletters and sermons.

Large metropolitan newspapers always have more news releases than they can publish. If they decide to publish your news release, they will edit it. If they decide to make it a feature article, they will phone you for more details and direct quotes. Always submit news releases to them anyway. You could get lucky with a feature story.

Small newspapers must have material to print, and they usually are short of manpower to gather, edit, and write stories. They will welcome well written news releases and articles especially with black and white glossy photographs.

## *The News Release Form*

Send all news releases on church letterhead. It may be the original or a copy of the news release copied on letterhead when you submit it to more than one news source.

Begin the copy four spaces below the church masthead and double space for newspapers and triple space for radio, using only one side of a page. Begin with the date, then the church contact person's name with their office and home phone number. Then type in your title with the "hook" that will grab the editor's interest.

Indent all paragraphs with a one inch margin around the copy. Do not use hyphenated words at the end of a line.

Finish a paragraph on the same page of copy using single space if necessary.

If the copy is two or more pages type in the word "More" at the bottom of the first page.

Number the pages with a hyphen and the subject of the news release on the top line of the next page (Page two - title of the news release.)

Use simple language and short sentences. Keep paragraphs short, four to five lines.

Keep news releases to one page if possible and no more than two pages at the maximum. Editors always have more copy and less space than they need. They do not have time to edit all copy.

End your news release with the word "End" at the bottom of the last page.

To submit a news release or article, call the daily or weekly newspaper to find out their deadline for news releases.

Daily newspapers usually have a "Religion and Ethics Page" editor with set times to submit the copy.

For news releases aimed at other than the religion editor of a daily newspaper, be careful not to release a news story to a daily newspaper or radio or television station that will "scoop" the other media. If you can, release the story to a weekly newspaper to match the same deadline as other media. For example, the weekly newspaper publishes on Friday and their deadline is Tuesday. Give your article to them on Tuesday. Give the news release for the daily media on Thursday so all articles will appear at the same time. Editors do not like to be "scooped."

## Photographs Can Make a Difference

Large metropolitan newspapers usually have between twenty and thirty photographers on their staff. They usually will not use photographs brought to them from other sources. They will take their own photos of your event if they cover it. However, you might include a small glossy print with your story to enhance your news release.

Weekly newspapers usually have one overworked photographer. They will be happy to receive glossy black and white photos from you. When you are taking photographs don't stand too far away from your subjects.

In a meeting, don't be afraid to walk up to the front of the audience and take a photograph of the speaker at the beginning of the program or arrive early and stage the speaker's photo. Professionals will stage even the most action packed photo. I saw a skate board photo with a boy in mid-air. He, his skate board, and his scarf were held up by wires with a fan blowing for action. Don't be afraid to stage your photos by telling people where to stand and which way to look.

Take two or three photographs of each pose to make sure that nobody blinked at the wrong time and that the facial expressions are all good. I usually take two and then say just one more. That usually breaks the tension and everyone smiles naturally.

If two weekly newspapers overlap your distribution area, be sure to give each of them a different pose of the event.

Some photos that all newspapers will use are head and shoulder photos of a guest speaker. Ask the speaker for a black and white glossy photo several weeks before the event. Copies of photos are easily made and the original can be returned to the speaker. Never submit color photos to newspapers. They can not use them.

Captions are important. Use a left to right method for naming individuals in all photos. Double space your photo captions and attach them to the back of the photo with the names showing below the photo. Always put the name and phone number of the contact person on the caption.

When taking photos, don't limit yourself to just having people looking at the camera. If it is a presentation, have them look at the presenter not at the camera. Try to make photos dramatic in some way with the subjects doing something. If you are taking the photos for the church newsletter take them with the people looking at the camera. Church members like to see their faces.

In order not to offend anyone that would not like to have their picture taken, I usually ask a group if anyone objects to having their photograph printed in the newspaper. If this is the case, I then ask them to leave the group before the photo is taken. This avoids problems later.

## *Local Monthly Magazines Reach People*

In many areas, monthly magazines for specific groups carry local articles and current events columns. This can be another media that features special church programs.

The most important information that you will need for sending news releases to a magazine is the name of the column, their deadline and publication date. This requires that you write your news release several weeks before you release it to the other media.

If you want to submit an article to a monthly magazine, send it to the editor several weeks before the magazine deadline. This will give the editor time to decide where the article will be featured, and if a photograph needs to be taken by his photographer. I sent an article to a monthly magazine three weeks before their deadline. The editor approved the article and sent a photographer to the church for a photo.

Be sure your article is something that will be of interest to the magazine's target audience.

If your article would be of general interest to other churches, don't forget to submit it to your denominational magazine. National denominational magazines do not work on deadlines for general articles and it may take several months before it will be published or rejected.

## *Radio Public Relations*

Many radio stations have news departments and appreciate receiving local news items. They sometimes send reporters to cover news stories, but they more often prefer phone interviews.

News releases you send to the newspapers will also be acceptable for radio. The only thing to keep in mind is not to release your story to the electronic media too soon. If they scoop the newspaper, you are in danger of the newspaper not running your story. Send your release to the radio station the same day the daily newspaper receives it.

Reporter coverage by radio is possible but not probable, unless your story is earth shaking. Usually the radio news director will want to have a telephone interview at the time of the event. Add a sentence to your news release stating that you can arrange for a telephone interview with the speaker and you will make the arrangements if the radio station desires it.

Community bulletin boards on radio stations are common. Usually it is for minor news events, but it is good coverage. Send them the items that you think will interest their listeners.

Remember radio is audio. They like anything with sound connected to it. If they can get some noise in the background for an interview, they love it. Radio is a good source for getting your story to the people.

Radio Public Service Announcements are effective, and they are easy to write and produce. The only thing to remember is that you have to warm up the listener's ear before you give them the message you want them to hear. Start all radio PSAs with some phrase that will get the listener to start thinking about what you are going to present to them. Ask a question. Make a statement. Always phrase your opening remark to get a positive response. An example might be: *"It isn't easy raising children today. A Positive*

*Parenting Course is planned to begin Tuesday evening ... "* You can, explain something about the program and end with where, when, and how to get more information about it. You might repeat the church's address and phone number because often people do not hear it the first time.

Radio PSAs can be ten, twenty or thirty seconds in length. Some radio stations use only ten second spots. Others prefer twenty or thirty second spots. You might send them one of each length about the same program on two pages then they can choose which one they prefer.

Never split a word at the end of a line, or put one public service announcement spot on two different sheets of paper. When you write numbers, spell out all numbers under ten and when you have large numbers write them phonetically like "100 thousand people."

A general guideline for the number of words for a PSA is: ten seconds about 25 words; twenty seconds 50 to 55 words; and thirty seconds; 70 to 75 words. Put "End" at the end of a spot so the announcer knows when to stop reading. If you write copy that goes to more than one page write "More" at the bottom of the first page.

If you decide to produce some PSAs call the public service director and ask if they will air your PSAs and what kind of PSAs they prefer. They may require an individual to come to the station and cut a tape. This is a matter of reading your PSA into a microphone; otherwise they will tell you to send them a written PSA announcement.

Be sure to send letters of appreciation to the station manager to thank him and the Public Service Director by name for your PSAs. Be sure to include, *"We have heard many favorable comments about the PSA or news release heard on your station."*

Radio interview programs can be fun.

Talk shows require a person who is at ease answering questions and expressing themselves to a large audience. Hosts like controversial subjects for discussions and people from other than the local area.

Interview shows without an audience are more numerous than talk shows and the hosts book the person about thirty days in advance. They will welcome just about any subject that will help their audience. The air times are often very early in the morning but the interviews are taped. You will never know how many people you can reach.

For any information about interview shows contact the Public Service Director of the station.

### *Television Public Relations*

The television news release is important but most television stations have their own news departments. They like to cover action news events. They do not like what they call "talking heads" or just interviews with individuals. Their specialty is covering colorful events and activities. They have a weakness for children. You might try having them cover some unusual visual Daily Vacation Bible School activity or a children's choir at Christmas time.

They will cover out-of-town speakers and famous people as talking heads on their news program. They like to cover the event while it is going on. They seldom run a story before the event.

Release your story at the same time you release it to the daily newspaper because if either scoops the other it's finished. Give them both the same break at the same time.

The television news team usually decides which stories they will cover at about 3:00pm the preceding afternoon. Be sure to get your news release to them prior to that time and hand deliver it to the station if possible. Do not send a news release too early to the TV station or it may get lost. About three days before the event is soon enough.

Sometimes TV stations will have a daily bulletin board. You can find out what the deadline is by calling the station.

TV Public Service Announcements are effective. The TV PSA is similar to the radio PSA as to the number of words, except that something visual is necessary. Before you decide to create a TV PSA, call the station's Public Service Director, and ask if they can use a PSA created by you. After you have explained what you would like to do, the PSA Director will probably volunteer to create the TV announcement for you. If the station creates a TV PSA spot for you they will send copies of the video tape to other TV stations in your city as a courtesy. You might ask the Public Service Director if this is possible.

Be sure to thank them by sending a letter to the station manager that includes their name.

### *Cultivate Your Local Media People*

While most of the local media news appears on its merit, it is important to cultivate your local media people. All media people appear to be busy. This is their way of life and although many things seem to be going on, they will almost always make time to see you. Remember, it is people like you that keep information flowing to them. Without you, the media couldn't exist. About 90 percent of everything you see and read in the media comes from news releases.

The best time to talk with media people depends on the type of media they represent. For weekly newspapers, usually Fridays; daily morning newspapers is between 2:00 and 3:00 p.m; radio and TV media people is usually from 9:00 to 10:00 a.m. When you visit them, ask for any advice they may have about publicizing your program. Be sure to leave your card and a brochure about your church. Keep contacts with media people short.

Creating a good public image of the church can do more for the outreach of a church than any other activity.

### *An Internet Web Site*

The internet is becoming a primary source of information for millions of people. Before I completed a computer course I felt that small churches should not create an internet website because of the cost of creating it and the complications of updating it.

Then my grand daughter and her husband on a small farm in Iowa sent me their website address. They have a static website with several links that do not have to be updated. They also have a monthly blog for their customers. I thought every church could develop a static website and they could use the website address in their publicity to help anyone know about their church.

It is not a great expense to create a website nor does it have to be updated all the time. It is easy to have a link to a monthly blog for church news.

I suggest that if you do not know how to create a website, you seek the advice of a computer teacher in your community. The computer teacher will know how to help you and give you the necessary advice to make it happen.

# Chapter Fourteen

## *Reaching the Unchurched in an Inexpensive, Minimum-Effort, Non-threatening Way*

This is an account of how one church reached the unchurched in their community in an inexpensive, minimum-effort, non-threatening way.

It's not easy reaching the unchurched in any community. Evangelism seminars and conferences try to prepare individuals to talk with people about their Christian faith. While some people are comfortable calling on the unchurched and talking with them, there are many people who will not do it.

Some churches report that they make phone calls to visitors immediately after they visit their church to welcome them. Other churches have area captains that call on visitors before the next Sunday and suggest that they meet before the Worship Service. I have heard of members of other churches who take visitors a loaf of homemade bread to welcome them. A hand written note by a pastor mailed during the week is impressive to the visitor. I have heard from people who received a hand written note from me that this was the reason they returned to visit again and became a regular visitor and member.

These are good ways to reach the visitors but what about reaching the shut-ins or the people recovering from hospitalizations or those who are handicapped in some way, whether physically, emotionally or socially, and the unchurched that never go to church? How can we reach these unchurched people who need the Lord and the Good News of The Gospel? Everyone in our church began praying daily for a way that we might reach these people who need the love, forgiveness and hope of our Lord.

Our small church found a way to reach the unchurched in our community with the Good News of The Gospel in our community in a simple, inexpensive, minimum-effort, non-threatening way that any church can duplicate in their community.

This is what happened. I called on a depressed elderly widow. I was worried about her. The next day I phoned her to see how she was feeling. She said, *"I'm so glad you called. I wish I could hear your voice everyday. You cheer me up!"* I told her that I was sorry but with my work schedule that wouldn't be possible. During my morning devotions God spoke to me. Why not use a telephone answering machine that would allow her to hear my voice everyday with a Scripture, a thought for the day, and a prayer.

I called the only church in San Diego with "Dial-A-Prayer" and asked them about the equipment and cost of recording their program. I found out how much a single telephone line to the church would cost. I presented the idea to the Board and they approved it.

After securing a commercial telephone answering machine and arranging for a separate DIAL HOPE telephone line we were ready to begin our ministry. We called it <u>The DIAL HOPE Telephone Outreach Ministry</u>. A caller hears a recorded Scripture, a thought for the day, a prayer, and an invitation to request prayer and visit a Sunday Service. The message is changed daily except Saturdays and holidays. It takes one person about two hours to record the daily devotionals for a week.

We used news releases to local newspapers, flyers, and our church newsletters to publicize DIAL HOPE. We had DIAL HOPE business cards printed for members to give to friends and acquaintances and we placed a free classified ad in a weekly newspaper.

It began happening!

People were calling in and requesting prayer. We began listing the prayer requests on the back of our Sunday Bulletins so that everyone could pray for them during the week. Our weekly prayer group prayed for them and I added them to my personal prayer list.

DIAL HOPE became the personal outreach ministry of every member of the church as they handed the DIAL HOPE business cards to people.

After two years, I was trying to find something for our June newsletter. I wondered how many DIAL HOPE calls we had had over the past two years. I multiplied the average number of daily calls, and was surprised to find that we had had 10,000 calls and about 500 prayer requests.

I asked the members how many calls they thought we had received. They guessed about one or two thousand calls. When I told them 10,000 calls they couldn't believe it!

I thought if we, a small church with only 65 members, could do it, any church could do it. I decided to write a "How To Do It DIAL HOPE Manual." I included in the manual what equipment was required and how to use it, suggestions for how to record the devotionals, and the day-to-day operations. I also included details on how to publicize the program, suggestions on how to write scripts, news releases, ads, and comply with copyright laws. I wanted the church to publish the manual but the denominational office was afraid of potential liability problems and denied permission.

My wife and I knew that DIAL HOPE was a proven, simple, inexpensive and non-threatening way for any church to reach the unchurched in their community with help, strength, and the hope of our Lord. We decided we would publish the DIAL HOPE Manual to help other churches do it without making all the mistakes we had made in setting it up.

We secured copyright permission to use the devotionals from a number of companies as well as Bible publishers. We sent articles to religious magazines and many of them were published.

Several churches made the DIAL HOPE Ministry a project for a volunteer group, a woman's group, the Deacons, or the Board members. (Individuals recorded two weeks of devotionals at a time.)

After ten years, 135 churches in 35 States and Canada had The DIAL HOPE Manual with a potential of 500 thousand calls and 50 thousand prayer requests annually. We couldn't believe it! Our small church had begun an outreach ministry that touched the lives of thousands of people everyday!

Our DIAL HOPE Ministry is still happening! Over

the past ten years we have had 50 thousand calls, and about five thousand requests for prayer.

Some of the kinds of prayer requests we have received over the years have been: *"I'm a single mother with three children studying for a law degree, pray for me"..."My daughter needs peace, please pray for her"..."I'm nine years old. My aunt had an operation, pray for her"... "I'm in pain, pray for me,"..."I'm beginning a new job, pray for me,"..."You kept me from having a nervous breakdown."* One of the most memorable prayer requests was, *"I can't s'eep because of anxiety and panic attacks. I saw your ad in the newspaper and I called. Thank you so much."* After a few seconds of silence, *"It's three o'clock. I got my husband's Bible and began reading the Psalms. It's not like yours, but it is helping me. I hope you don't mind me calling your machine."* There was a few more seconds of silence. *"It's 4:30. I'm calmed down now. Everyone is asleep. I can go to sleep now. I want you to know that I'm recovering from drugs and alcohol. After listening to you, I have hope again. You helped me to continue my nineteen months of sobriety. I almost lost it tonight. Thank you again for your message. Pray for me."*

Some letters we received from people who have called DIAL HOPE include:

> "I appreciate your DIAL HOPE prayer line very much. Because of my health, I am not able to go to church, so DIAL HOPE is a real blessing."

> "For some time now, I have been listening to DIAL HOPE, sometimes quietly and prayerfully, sometimes frantically when my profuse and unpredictable sinus condition, or some other problem demonstrates the frailty of the human condition and my heart is beating too fast from fear. Always the message has helped me to regain

an inner equilibrium and to focus on higher levels of being. I don't think anyone should listen without a pen in hand to capture some of the jewels for later reflection."

"One day looking for help in the phone book, I found you under DIAL HOPE. You truly have been a candle in the pitch blackness when I was so low I had to look up to see my toes. The readings are so uplifting. I keep you on re-dial on my telephone. A million thanks aren't enough for the aid you've given me."

"Sometimes things are difficult, and we need help to live through them. Not everything works out the way we plan, but we need to keep trying. It's so good to be able to reach out for help and receive it. I give thanks! After just one ring, a familiar voice on the other end offers reassurance. I am connected with help to guide me. The calmness, understanding, and the power of prayer, makes everything okay; my weakness is overcome, I am given strength. I cannot thank you enough, but I do not understand how it is that when the DIAL HOPE message is changed daily, each time I call it, it seems my troubles are addressed and answered. I trust in all you say and my faith grows. I wonder if others benefit as much as I? You make life wonderful!"

"Life has difficulties. Tough problems can wake us at 2:30 in the morning. DIAL HOPE is available at all times for the urgent need to regain faith that things will get better with God's guidance. You reach handicapped people, troubled people, people living far from your church, working people, retired people, elderly people, and others who are confined and need the Word of God to uplift them. Thanks a million!"

Some pastors and lay persons who have begun a DIAL HOPE ministry in their church write: "DIAL HOPE is one of the most rewarding programs of my thirty year ministry. We've only been in the program a few months... In the first month, we had eighty-four requests for prayer! It is certainly meeting a need in this area."

"As you know, we are just getting started (with DIAL HOPE,) but the calls are coming in and we have visions of six telephones ringing constantly and helping immeasurably."

"I want to thank you for Tuesday's message. As I was listening, my years of resistance to God melted away, and I surrendered myself to Christ. I feel like a new person now."

"I am a member of a small church located away from several towns. We often comment that we are not located near people who need our help. DIAL HOPE is an excellent solution for our congregation's need to help others."

While on a vacation tour of Bulgaria, I had one free afternoon in Plovdiv, the second largest city in Bulgaria. I asked the hotel concierge to phone a Protestant Church. The only person in the church that spoke English answered the phone. He came to the hotel and took me to the church. He told me that the church had lost many members under communism and it was difficult to reach the unchurched.

I told him about DIAL HOPE. When I returned to the United States, I sent him a DIAL HOPE Manual. He wrote that the church was beginning a DIAL HOPE Ministry. He is translating the manual into Bulgarian and will share it with other Protestant Churches in Bulgaria.

The DIAL HOPE Manual is included in the appendix of this book should you like to begin a DIAL HOPE telephone outreach ministry in your church.

It's amazing what God can do with a few dedicated people and limited means!

*Never underestimate the power of God!*

### A Pastor's Personal Public Relations

Normally Public Relations refer to corporations and organizations. Since a pastor's personality and ministry are major factors in a church's public relations, it is important to think of a pastor's personal public relations as one of the most important aspects in a church's outreach ministry.

Everything a pastor says or does affects the church's image in the eyes of the members and the unchurched of a community. Every pastor begins his or her ministry with the idea of doing everything perfectly, then the "shovel breaks," and slowly the pastor learns what to do and what not to do.

On my second base in the Air Force, I had some problems in my ministry. A Staff Chaplain scheduled an inspection visit. I thought, *"Now I'll get some answers about what to do about my problems."*

When he arrived I began dumping my load of problems. The Staff Chaplain sat back in his chair and listening intently. After I finished he said, *"Well, on some bases you'll learn what to do, and some bases you'll learn what not to do. It looks like you are learning what not to do on this base."* In other words he was saying that I would have to learn by experience what to do and what not to do.

After a career as a chaplain and pastor, I have had many good and bad experiences doing my personal public relations ministry. I would like to share some of the "what to do" ways of doing personal ministry that enhances the public relations of a pastor and a church.

Since every church and community is different, I offer the following suggestions that may or may not help you with your ministry. It is my hope that some of the following chapters will keep the "what not to do" to a minimum.

# Chapter Fifteen

## *Personalizing Funeral and Wedding Services*

For many years, I didn't have a clue as to how to make a funeral or memorial service meaningful and personal to those who loved the person who had gone on to Glory. I merely used the order of worship in the Book of Common Worship. I sensed something was missing but I didn't know how to fix it.

Then one day it dawned on me. A memorial or funeral service should be a time when everyone has an opportunity to express how they feel about the person who had touched their lives in some wonderful way.

Looking back over my ministry I only wish someone had shown me how to do it years ago. I hope some of these ideas will help other pastors with their memorial and funeral services.

When I meet with the members of the family to plan the memorial or funeral service, I find out what special arrangements and thoughts they would like to have included in the service. If I do not know the person, I ask about his or her life.

If it is a memorial service, I suggest that they bring pictures and any meaningful mementos of their loved one. I place them on a table at the front of the sanctuary.

Then I ask those making the arrangements to ask all the members of the family to write about some happy memories they have of their beloved that I might read or that they may wish to share during the service. I also suggest that they contact friends of the person and ask them to write some happy memory that I might read or that they might share during the service. I ask them to bring their written memories to me just before the service.

I always arrive early for the service and greet everyone personally. I tell them that I'm officiating and that we will be having a time during the service for anyone to stand where they are and share a happy memory of the person. This encourages some of them to participate.

Since we are honoring the person I feel that it doesn't matter how long the memories take. The important thing is that we share our thoughts about how much the person meant to us. I have had services when the memory time has taken about five minutes and other times when it took twenty minutes. It is important for individuals to have the opportunity to share their wonderful memories.

I always begin the sharing time with my own personal observations. Even when I didn't know the person, I take what the family members tell me about the person when we are planning the service and I say, "I didn't know (the person's name) personally, but I have been told etc." Then I say, "I wish I had had the opportunity to know (him or her.)"

I usually ask people in the audience to share their memories first and then I have the family share their thoughts or I read their thoughts last.

Before I begin the service I ask the loved ones if all the members of the family are present. If not, I wait until they arrive. They are usually all present.

I keep the order of worship simple and include what the family desires.

I begin by saying, "We are gathered here in a celebration of love for _____. We are here to tell _____ that we love you and we will always remember you." This is followed with a call to worship and a prayer.

A hymn is optional at this time.

I read the formal obituary from the newspaper followed with "Hear words of comfort from the Old Testament" (I read parts of Psalm 46 and the entire 23rd Psalm.)

Then I say, "Now is a time to share some happy memories. We are all friends of _____ and we don't have to be bashful about sharing some happy memories of _____. It can be just a statement of what _____ meant to you. Just stand up where you are and share some of your thoughts with us. Then I begin by sharing my thoughts. Usually someone will volunteer to share their thoughts, if not, I read something that was given to me by someone other than the family and ask for volunteers again. Give them time. They will respond.

After everyone has had their say, I call on the family members to express their thoughts or I read what the family members have given me.

Next I say, "Hear the words of comfort from the New Testament."

(I Corinthians 15: 20-22; I Thessalonians 4:13 &14; Revelation 21:1a,3b, & 4; then I finish with John 14: 1-4, 6, 25-27.)

Next is a time for a solo, poetry, a devotional and/or a

hymn followed by a prayer for the loved one gone to Glory.

My prayer is "Our Loving Heavenly Father, receive your servant _____ for (he or she) returns to you. May (he/she) hear your words of welcome, 'Come, you blessed of my Father, and receive the unfading crown of glory.' May the angels surround (him/her) and welcome (him/her) in peace. Into your hands we commend _____. Receive (him/her) into the joys of your heavenly home. May (he/she) and all the departed rest in peace. Amen."

Then I pray a prayer of committal, "Unto the mercy of Almighty God, we commend the soul of our (brother/sister) departed in the sure and certain hope of the resurrection to eternal life through Jesus Christ Our Lord, Amen."

I continue saying a closing prayer for all the members of the church who have departed loved ones, the loved ones of the person we honor, and conclude with the Lord's Prayer followed by the Benediction.

I pay my respects to the family, and then go to the entrance to shake hands with everyone as they leave.

### Graveside Committal Service

I use the same service and omit the hymns, poetry, and devotionals, etc, for a graveside service.

These are only my suggestions for pastors to use or not as they desire, within the doctrines of their church. I only hope that some of these ideas might help some pastor with his or her ministry.

### Making Marriage Ceremonies Personal

Often marriage ceremonies are completely formal without any mention of the personal lives of the couple.

If the formal ceremony is the preference of the pastor, then it should remain formal.

If a pastor would like to make the marriage ceremony personal for the couple and their guests, I have some suggestions that may be helpful.

When the couple contacts the pastor to make arrangements for the wedding, and after the pastor has given them premarital counseling, the pastor might suggest that they each write how they met, what their feelings were when they first met, and how they felt during their courtship.

Then during the ceremony, after the formal beginnings and before they pledge their troth, the pastor may shares excerpts from their written memories.

This provides some personal thoughts of the bride and groom that will bring personal insights into their lives and be enjoyed by everyone.

Of course the couple may wish to write and share their own vows, which adds to the personal nature of the wedding.

### A Blended Family Ceremony
### Immediately Following the Wedding

Since many divorced people with children remarry, I have originated a Family Dedication Service in order to include the children in the formation of the new family. I hope this service might prove helpful for families, and for pastors who officiate at these marriages. (This ceremony is only a suggestion and may or may not be what a family may desire.)

### A Family Dedication Service

Families have always been important to our way of life. As we have united (first names of bride and groom) in the bond of marriage, so we will now unite their family in love. We will ask (the first names of the children) to join (the first names of the married couple). As (first names of married couple) have pledged their love to each other, now we will have all of the members of this new family pledge their love to each other and to God.

Do all of you promise to be loyal and faithful to your new family?

Each member will respond: "I will."

When there are problems, do you promise to help the other members of your new family in any way that you are able?

"I will."

Do all of you promise to do everything you can to bring love and harmony to your family?

"I will."

Will you seek God's help with your life and the life of your new family?

"I will."

(Each member of the family will be given a candle. The candles will be lit. Small children can be helped and/or held by a step-family member. A large unlit candle is placed on a table. Each member's candle is lit.)

Now as a symbol of your love and unity as a family, I ask each of you to take the candle representing you; and all of you light the large candle representing your new family. After you have lit the family candle, you will blow out your candle to indicate that you have pledged your love and loyalty to your new family.

(If this is an evening ceremony, after each family member lights their candle, have the lights of the room turned out. The pastor could have a flashlight in order to read the closing prayer or the pastor may want to offer an extemporaneous prayer.)

Let us pray.

Our loving Heavenly Father, we ask Your blessing upon this new family. Help them to live together in love, forgiveness, and understanding of each other's needs, and desires. Give them strength, and guidance, as they meet life's problems. Help them to grow together in love and happiness. Bless them and help them, we pray, in Jesus' name. Amen.

(After the lights have been turned on.)

Ladies and gentlemen, I present to you the new _____family!

(Have the family hug. A hug, and a single rose are given to each of the mother-in-laws by each of the children.)

The Benediction

The grace of Christ attend you. The love of God surround you. The Holy Spirit keep you, that you may live in faith. Always have hope, and grow in love with one another both now and forever more. Amen.

Before you use this service be sure to read the entire service to everyone in the new family to make sure that everyone, including the children, approves of the service.

# Chapter Sixteen

## *Suggestions to Help Create Happy Marriages*

It isn't easy being married. Everyone comes to marriage from different backgrounds and has to make adjustments from a single life. Singles can do what they want to, when they want to, without thinking about anyone else. Suddenly they have to think about someone else - their wants, desires, goals, and way of life - and how to adjust to the other person in many ways.

The marriage relationship requires love, dedication, caring, constant concern, responsibility, help and understanding.

Pastors have a unique opportunity to help singles contemplating marriage, premarital and marital counseling, with ideas in sermons and marriage enrichment classes.

Through practical experience and study, I have developed fifteen suggestions that may be helpful for pastors. For public relations and publicity, I have used the individual suggestions as attention grabbers in news releases to newspapers and all fifteen suggestions summarized to one sentence each for flyers to the general public for marriage class promotions.

The following are the fifteen suggestions, including illustrations that may help others understand the suggestions.

1. Men and women generally think differently. Men tend to think objectively in terms of the facts and women tend to think subjectively in terms of themselves. There may be some exceptions in some cases.

An example could be used by the pastor. He might suggest that a couple may decide to drive to New York City. Ask the couple: "What will the man do?" Usually the man will say he has to have the car checked, figure the mileage, make reservations for every night, etc,. Ask "What will the woman do?" Usually a woman will think of what clothes to wear and take with her and say, "Let's go!"

Another example might be a couple that visits another couple. They walk into the other couple's house and the man says, "You really have a nice house." The pastor could ask, "What will the woman be thinking?" Usually she will be thinking "What's the matter with our house?" or "Don't you like our house?" She may even ask her husband later, "Don't you like our house?" To the man he is just giving a compliment to the other couple. He doesn't want their house but now he has a problem with his wife and often he can't understand why his wife is upset. It is a simple misunderstanding because a man tends to think objectively and his wife thinks subjectively. It is important for the wife to ask the husband what he means when she feels her husband is upset and vice versa in order to come to an understanding. I always warn the man during a counseling session, "Don't compliment a mutual lady friend on her clothes in the presence of his wife unless he wants to spend a lot of money when his wife goes out and buys a new outfit."

In each case the man is thinking objectively while his wife is thinking subjectively about her house, her clothes, etc,. This difference in the ways of thinking can cause many problems for any couple. If it happens ask your mate what he or she meant by what was said. Communicate by asking, "Why?"

2. The Bible states "Do not let the sun go down on your wrath" (Ephesians 4:26). Settle differences as soon as possible. If you have a difference of opinion, after everyone calms down, talk about it. Ask why? Listen and talk it out. Don't let an offense fester or it will grow and damage your marriage. Compromise, say you are sorry. Your love is more important than a problem.

3. Communication is the basis of a good relationship. Do not refuse to talk. Share your feelings. Make a rule that it is O.K. to say anything and that you will still love each other no matter what is said.

Some people refuse to talk if they are upset about something. They will not tell their mate what is wrong and they get angry because their mate does not satisfy their need. How can a mate respond if he or she doesn't know what's wrong? It is better for a person to "blow up" and get their feeling out than to keep them "pent up" inside. Pent up feelings can turn into all kinds of problems including physical, emotional, or mental problems. Communicate with your mate for good health.

4. You will know when your mate is tired or emotionally drained. He or she may go on a rampage and say

the most cutting things. They may turn into an obnoxious person. Don't fight with them. Give them space and let them alone. Say to them, "Let's get a good night's sleep and we'll talk about it tomorrow." After a time of rest and relaxation if you are the one who yelled and screamed tell your mate you're sorry and you didn't mean it. Allow for each other's feelings.

5. Plan for breaks in your routine of living. Plan to go out one night a week together even when you have children. Plan on a special event once a month that you can look forward too, a short trip, a special show, taking the children on a new experience. Have a good time together.

6. Plan one big trip every year. Save for it and read up on the area. A change of scenery can perk up your life. Nothing is more valuable than creating happy memories together.

My wife and I have concentrated on creating happy memory trips all through our marriage. We once saved for three years in order to take our family on a trip around Europe. Often now when we watch a television program set in a foreign country those memories flood our minds and bring us closer together.

7. Try to help your mate achieve something he or she wants to do in life. If this means working around the house to make it happen do it. As you make each other happy you will be happy.

When we married, I was a senior in college following three years as a rifleman on the front lines during WWII. Betty was a freshman. She wanted to finish college while I was in seminary. I held down three part time jobs to help her graduate at the same time I graduated from seminary. When she graduated, I pinned an orchid on her graduation gown and said, "Now, I've set you free. You have your degree and you will always be able to get a good position if anything happens to me." At the same time, she helped me through seminary by typing my papers, playing the piano for my student pastorate church services and calling on the members. Throughout our lives we have helped each other in many ways which has strengthened our love for each other. Help your mate achieve their dreams and it will help create a happy marriage.

8. Set realistic goals you want to accomplish. Think about what you want to accomplish in one year, five years, and ten years. Write your goals on paper. Outline how you will achieve your goals. Put them where you can read them often. As you achieve your goals you will enjoy your life and it will bring you and your mate closer together.

In our case, when we were seriously considering marriage, we began setting our goals. I was planning to become a chaplain in the Air Force and I knew I would have to complete three years of seminary. Our one year goal was to move to the seminary and we would enroll in the two schools. Our five year goal was for both of us to graduate. I would be commissioned in the Air Force and Betty would teach on bases where I was assigned. Our ten year goal was to begin our family. We accomplished all three goals and added the details as we progressed toward those goals.

For some couples the goals may be to save for a down payment on a house or to take a trip or to do something they have wanted to do all their lives. Whatever it is it is important to set and accomplish goals in marriage to strengthen the bond of marriage and create happiness for both mates.

9. Talk out minor irritations with your mate. No one is

a mind reader and they can't make adjustments unless they know what to adjust to.

Everyone has minor habits that may drive their mate "bonkers." I cannot stand anyone tearing paper. My wife likes to tear every unimportant paper into tiny pieces. She likes to squeeze the toothpaste tube in the center and I like to roll it up from the end. We talked it over. She doesn't tear paper around me and we bought two toothpaste tubes to keep the peace. We continue to talk and act on our irritations.

10. Never try to hurt one another no matter what the circumstance. You can hurt your mate at any time. You know how to hurt your mate. You can trigger a fight any time you want to. Don't do it.

We made a pact early in our marriage that we would try never to hurt each other and especially in the presence of other people. Nothing is more devastating to an individual or a marriage than for another couple to have a verbal fight in public. We have witnessed a married couple verbally fighting in our presence. It not only hurt the couple but it put an end to our relationship with that couple. Don't do it. Everyone suffers.

11. When you verbally fight do not use past mistakes to hurt your mate. Don't use parent's mistakes to hurt your mate. Stay in the present here and now.

Every couple will have differences of opinion that will cause verbal fights unless one of the mates is a doormat for the other and they never express their opinions.

The most difficult thing for a mate in a verbal fight is for one mate to bring up some mistake that happened in the past. The mate may have apologized and done everything in his or her power to make amends. Then later in a verbal fight they accuse the other mate of doing it again.

There is nothing the other mate can do to change the past. "That's what you always do. Remember when you did that five years ago? You never change!" or "You act that way because your dad or mother treated you that way and you will always be that way." People can and do change. You probably have changed during the past ten years and so can your mate.

Don't play the blame game. Verbally fight in the here and now. Talk about the present disagreement and how you can solve it. Don't call each other names.

If everything fails and sometimes it happens in every marriage, I always tell the husband, "Be sure you have the key to the front door in your pocket if you "storm" out of the house because I had to crawl back in through a bathroom window when it happened to me."

No matter what happens as soon as possible say you are sorry and make amends. Every marriage goes through verbal fights. Don't be alarmed. Find a way to mend the marriage.

12. Many times in marriage, couples take each other for granted. They go through the routine of living without reminding each other of their love for each other. There is something to be said for saying something out loud. It not only reminds the person who says it of their feelings but it is also reassuring for the person who hears it. This is why some couples renew their marriage vows on their 25th wedding anniversary. Do it. Tell your mate you love them everyday.

Everyone wants to be appreciated for what they do in life. This is true in a marriage as well. A wife likes to be thanked for a good meal. A husband likes to be thanked for taking his wife shopping. Thank each other for anything the other mate does for you.

After Betty does something for me and I don't respond, she often whimsically smiles and says to me, "Thank you Betty for doing that thing for me." You will be surprised how much this means in creating a happy marriage.

13. We have said some horrible things to each other when we've been tired or upset during our 59 years of marriage, but one thing that has kept our marriage alive and fun has been the fact that no matter what is said or done we love each other and we always will no matter what happens. We aren't afraid to apologize or accept the blame for anything and we "mend fences" as soon as possible.

Tell each other that this is a fact; "I will always be there for you no matter what happens. You can count on it." And then do it. Forgive each other no matter what happens.

14. No one is right all of the time. Everyone makes mistakes. When we realize that we are all human beings and no one is perfect it will go a long way toward taking away guilt and the lowering of self esteem. Join the human race and don't blame yourself for your mistakes. Forgive yourself and forgive others and admit you are a human being and say you are sorry.

15. Life can get boring and routine. People often do the same things every day, see the same things every day, see the same people and think the same thoughts over and over again. Everyone needs to think new thoughts and get new ideas on how to live life. One of the simplest things a person can do to get some new thoughts and new ideas about living life is to attend a worship service every week. For thousands of years, people have been doing it. It has helped and continues to help people even today.

Think about it. It only takes one hour a week. Not only will you get some new thoughts about living life but you will find inspiration, help and strength. You will make friends that can help you, and your children will get basic moral beliefs that will help them face the temptations of youth.

Go "church shopping" and visit different churches until you find a church that helps you. Do it and it will help you create a happy marriage.

Don't think that anyone else will be a better mate for you. They are human and they will have imperfections too.

Many divorces today are caused because of temptation. Individuals think that someone else will make them a better mate. Protect your marriage by not putting yourself in a place where you might be tempted.

When I enlisted in the Army as a young man during WWII, my Dad an Army veteran of WWI and a pastor said, *"Son, you will face all kinds of temptations in the Army. I want to give you a verse in the Bible that will help you. Memorize it, and do it. You will be glad you did. The verse is 1 Corinthians 10:13. 'No Temptation has overtaken you except such as is common to man; but God is faithful, who will not allow you to be tempted beyond what you are able, but with the temptation will also make the way of escape, that you may be able to bear it.,'"* (New King James Version.)

Then Dad said, *"Everyone is tempted in the same ways, but God will make a way to escape. Son, run from every temptation. Nowhere in the Bible does it say to go to a temptation. In the Lord's Prayer it states, 'Lead us not into temptation.' Pick up your feet and run from temptation. Find something else to do during the times that you are tempted, like enrolling in a night school course or making something in a hobby shop. Do it, and you'll be glad you did."* I ran several times from temptations, and I'm glad I did. I still run from temptation.

You want to create a happy marriage? Do it. Run from temptations and you'll be glad you did.

Like anything else in life, if you want anything, it requires work. To create a happy marriage it takes love, work, dedication and responsibility. These fifteen suggestions are a way to do it. Do it and may God bless you.

# Chapter Seventeen

## *Helping Young People with the Three Greatest Choices of Their Lives*

During my Air Force Chaplaincy career I had an opportunity to help thousands of young men and women. At one time I was stationed at the only basic training center in the Air Force, Lackland Air Force Base in San Antonio, Texas.

Thousands of young men and women left civilian life to begin an entire new way of life on that base. Every month they, and every person in the Air Force, were required to attend a Character Guidance Lecture by a chaplain. From personal counseling sessions I realized that these young single men and women often had not thought about their futures. I decided to use a Character Guidance Lecture as a way of helping them plan their lives. I called my talk, "<u>The Three Greatest Choices of Your Life</u>."

Every time I met a group of these airmen, I asked them if they had seen me. If they hadn't seen me, I gave them my "talk." Five years after leaving Lackland Air

Force Base, I was in civilian clothes going through a cafeteria line in Japan. A young sergeant heard me ask for something and said, *"You were a chaplain at Lackland five years ago."* I said, *"Yes, I was stationed at Lackland."* Then he said, *"I heard your 'Three Greatest Choices in Life' talk. I did it, and it worked for me. Thank you."* I thanked him.

I repeated this talk for thousands of young people over my entire career and now I am sharing it with other pastors to help them help their young people.

## The Three Greatest Choices in Your Life

There are three major choices that everyone must make in their lives. Make good choices and you will be successful and happy. Let someone else make these choices for you and you may be frustrated and sorry. Either you will make these choices or life will make them for you.

The first choice is your lifelong career. Since you will spend most of your life on a job choose an occupation you enjoy. Someone may offer you a job that will pay well but if it's not what you want to do for the rest of your life turn it down and follow your dream.

Get as much education as you can. I worked my way through college as a district distributor for the Valley Times Newspaper for San Fernando Valley, California. Every day I distributed newspapers to stores and corner boys selling papers. When I graduated from college my boss offered me a position as manager of all The Valley Times newspapers distributed in Burbank, California. I would have made a huge salary and commissions. I had planned to go to seminary for three years and become a chaplain in the Air Force. I made my choice and went to seminary.

During my Air Force career I never made the money I could have made as a newspaper manager but I achieved a way of life that gave me meaning, purpose and a feeling of accomplishment that I could never have experienced as a newspaper manager. If I, as a young college graduate, had that same choice to make again, I would make the same decision all over again because it has given me the kind of life and a position so challenging and exciting that I always looked forward to going to work everyday.

Take time to think about your interests, your abilities, the possible occupations that would provide you with opportunities and a lifestyle that will bring meaning, purpose, and a feeling of accomplishment.

Make a list of the occupations that appeal to you. Then make appointments to talk with someone in that occupation to see what it is all about and what is required to enter that employment opportunity.

Don't sell yourself short on an occupation. You may be offered a job out of high school or college that may look good at the time, but if you get married and have a family you may sell yourself short on your abilities and get stuck in a job you don't like.

When I began going to college, one of the part time jobs I had was as a temporary mail carrier during the school year. One carrier told me that he had always wanted to go to college, but he got married and had two children. In order to support his family he became a mail carrier. He resented the fact that he never went to college. Of course, he could have gone to college at night, but he didn't.

My Dad told me, "Son, you can put your money in a car, a business or a house and in time any of these may become worthless. But put your time and money in education and no one can take it away from you. It will always help you with employment and living life."

I know that every day we read about self-made men and women who achieved success without going to college but they are the exceptions. For every person who succeeds without a college education, there are thousands who fail to become as successful as they desire.

If possible, get your education while you are single without the responsibilities of married life. However, married or divorced individuals with children, can secure the necessary education to progress in life if they choose to do it.

A divorcee with four children was a receptionist. She thought she was stuck in a low paying job for life. I suggested that she go to college part time and gradually she could improve her situation in life. She said, *"I've got four kids. How can I go to college?"* I asked her if she had neighbors with children. I suggested she swap babysitting nights with a neighbor and go to college two nights a week. After thinking it over, she decided to do it. Later, she also enrolled in Saturday classes. She majored in business administration, and was promoted gradually to personnel director. Ten years later, at the age of 38, she graduated with a Bachelor of Science degree in Business Administration and she was promoted to Vice President of Personnel. Since then, three of her four children went to college and she remarried.

No one is too old to get a college education. It's a matter of choice and determination.

Some young people think that they need to get a college education in four or five years but I always ask them if they would like to have a surgeon under the age of thirty operate on them or if they would like a lawyer under the age of thirty defend them on a serious charge in court? Then I say, *"If you don't complete your degree until the age of thirty, you will still have 35 or more years to benefit from your education in your chosen occupation."* Choose an occupation you enjoy.

Get as much education as you can and keep learning all through your life.

The second choice is your choice of a mate. Choose a mate that is compatible with your career choice, your desire for a family, and a way of life that meets both of your dreams.

As a senior in high school, I dated a girl that seemed to have similar ideals and values as mine. When we began thinking of marriage, I asked her what she wanted in a marriage. She said, *"I want to live in one place, have three children, have a husband that goes to work everyday, and I want to live in a white house with a picket fence."*

I said, *"That's not at all what I want in marriage. I want an occupation that will move me and my family to different places around the world. I don't care how many children I have and I don't care where I live."*

We realized that we had irreconcilable differences about marriage and we parted as friends. Twenty five years later, I met her again. She invited me, my wife and daughter to visit her family. She, her husband, and her three sons welcomed us. I said, *"Well I see you got everything you wanted; a white house with a picket fence, a husband that commutes to work everyday and three sons."* By that time, I had married a wonderful lady that loved to travel, had a daughter and had lived in California, Virginia, Germany, Holland, New Mexico, Texas, Okinawa, and Michigan. We had both fulfilled our marriage dreams.

It goes without saying that the "chemistry" between a couple has to be there for a marriage to be happy. To marry without the chemistry, or mutual attraction, is to court marital disaster.

Look for a mate where people with your ideals and values gather, like church, school, library, clubs or organizations. Choose a mate who is a responsible person; someone you can count on to help you; someone with similar goals, likes and dislikes; someone who would never hurt you. Your mate should be a person you enjoy being with and miss when you are apart. Make sure your mate fits your occupational choice. If your job requires that you and your family move every few years, don't choose a mate that wants to live in only one place. Agree on family and future plans. Use your head as well as your heart when you choose a mate.

The third choice is what values you want to live by. Don't get involved in destructive activities that can ruin your future like drugs, alcohol, permissive behavior and compulsive habits. Find help for living your life in time-tested ways like attending a church service once a week, reading a page a day in the Psalms, Proverbs and the New Testament, and praying asking God to help you everyday.

Think about it. What is one hour a week in the church of your choice? You will get some new thoughts about living life and you will meet people with your same values. Find the largest church youth group you can find and attend every week. After attending for six months, I met my wife in one of these groups. You can laugh at this suggestion, but pastors and churches have been helping people for hundreds of years and it's still happening. Think about it.

When I went into the Army as an infantry soldier in WWII, my preacher Daddy said, *"Son you will be tempted in many ways in the Army. Memorize this verse: I Corinthians 10:13."* Then he read it to me. He said, *"Run from all temptations. You will be glad you did."* Dad was right and I actually ran from temptations many times and I'm glad I did. It made a great difference in my life and I recommend it to you.

I Corinthians 10:13, (NKJV) states, *"No temptation has overtaken you except such as is common to man (and woman); but God is faithful, who will not allow you to be tempted beyond what you are able, but with the temptation will also make a way to escape, that you may be able to bear it."*

Run from all temptations. Put physical and mental distance between you and the temptation. When you are tempted, do something else like take a night school course, get involved in a hobby, a sport, or some other activity. Nowhere in the Bible does it say to go to a temptation. The Lord's Prayer states, *"Lead us not into temptation."*

Don't let your hormones, your peers, or anyone else make your decisions about how to live your life. Make your own choices and decisions and do it.

Think about what you want to be doing five, ten, or twenty years from today. List your goals and write out plans for how you are going to achieve them. Then *"Go for it!"* Circumstances may cause your plans to crash, but don't give up. Make some new plans. Modify your new plans and keep on pursuing your dreams. Every time you modify your plans or make new ones you will learn to plan better. You will also achieve your goals and you will have a successful life.

These three major choices in life will be made by you

or circumstances in life will make the choices for you. Life's choices may not be what you want to be doing or who you want to be sharing your life with, so make your own choices and live a happy successful life. It's your decision.

# Chapter Eighteen

## *Effective Healing and Hospital Ministry Techniques*

Some pastors are reluctant to pray for healing for individuals. They worry that if they pray for a person's healing, and then the person gets worse or dies, it is their fault because their faith wasn't strong enough.

Jesus said, "Ask and it will be given to you,"(Matthew 7:7 NKJV). He didn't limit what we should pray for. He also said "Again I say to you that if two of you agree on earth concerning anything that they ask, it will be done for them by my Father in heaven." (Matthew 18:19 NKJV)

We are to ask and let God decide the results.

The way I see it, we are like an adult child. Just as a parent would like to do things for his or her adult child, the parent can't do anything unless the child asks. This is our relationship with God.

I began praying specific prayers for healing while stationed at Langley Air Force Base in Virginia. It was my first assignment as a chaplain after completing college and seminary.

There was a small hospital on the base with about forty beds. We had enough chaplains that we were each given one day a week as hospital duty chaplain. Wednesday was my hospital duty chaplain day.

At 10:00 p.m. on a Wednesday evening, I was called to the hospital. A lady was dying. The doctors said she probably wouldn't live through the night. They had called her family members. They were gathered in the room next to hers. I brought my Bible and I read different passages of comfort for them and prayed with them. Since the lady was in the next room I thought I should pray for her to show the family that I cared.

She was in a coma under an oxygen tent. Her hand was on the covers. I took her hand and prayed out loud for her healing. I returned to the family and gave them my card and told them to call me if they needed me.

I didn't hear from them again and I figured that they had made some arrangements with the next day's hospital duty chaplain.

The following Wednesday I was making my rounds visiting patients in the hospital. I came to the lady's room and wondered who they had put in her room. I walked in and said, *"I'm Chaplain Hayward ..."* She interrupted me. She said, *"You're the chaplain who prayed for me! I was in a coma, but I heard your prayer, and I'm going to get well!"*

I couldn't believe it. I hadn't felt any power going through me and I thought that she had died. The lady recovered and she began attending my chapel services faithfully.

From that time on I always prayed for the healing of individuals even if they were terminal.

One time a lady said, *"My husband is terminally ill in the hospital, would you please visit him?"* I agreed to see him.

When I got to his room he had the TV turned on very loud. I introduced myself and over the blaring TV told him his wife had asked me to visit him. He didn't turn the TV volume down or pay any attention to me. It was impossible to talk with him. I finally said, *"I always pray with everyone I visit in the hospital, would you like to have me pray with you?"* He gave me his hand. I prayed for his healing over the blaring TV. Then I left.

Two weeks later, I saw his wife. I asked about her husband. She said, *"Oh he died during the night after you visited him."* Then she said, *"When I visited him that afternoon after you prayed with him, he was a changed man. He wasn't belligerent anymore. He was peaceful and happy to see me. I couldn't believe the change in him, Thank you for visiting him."* Sometimes the healing takes place in heaven.

I always tell everyone I pray for that Jesus said, *"Ask and you will receive."* He didn't limit what we can ask for. We ask and leave the results to God.

I've seen an 80 year old lady facing an operation. The doctors told her children that she probably wouldn't survive the operation. Her children asked me to pray with her. I went to her home the day before she was to go to the hospital. I prayed with her for a successful operation and for the doctors and nurses. She not only survived, but when the nurse asked her if she needed a pain pill she said "I don't have any pain." She continued to be an active member of the church for the next 10 years.

I've seen a lady with phobias overcome her fears through prayer. I prayed with her and she prayed every time she felt a fear coming on. I helped her through prayer and counseling. After a time her fears were gone.

I've seen a married couple turn what seemed a hopeless relationship into a stronger love through my prayers with them and their prayers for each other which gave them the confidence to make a new beginning. I continued to help them through prayer and counseling.

I've seen a person who hadn't been employed for many years get a job as a result of prayers with him and his own personal prayers and others praying for him to get a job. This changed his attitude and gave him the courage to do it.

Prayer is powerful and it can help individuals no matter what their situation in life.

I pray all the time and with everyone face to face or over the telephone. God hears and answers our prayers. Don't be afraid to pray and experience God's answer.

My suggestion for creating a healing ministry is to begin by asking individuals if they would like to have you pray with them about some particular problem, situation or condition. They will probably welcome your prayers.

As you no doubt already know you can pray anytime, anywhere and in any manner. Depending on the situation, I pray for individuals by just bowing my head and praying. Other times I stand behind them and place my hands on their shoulders or take their hands and pray. At other times we will kneel in prayer. If I am in the church office, I often take them into the sanctuary and kneel with them. I ask them to pray orally and if they say they don't know how to pray, I have them repeat a prayer after me. Then I pray for them.

Before my retirement, on Sundays, ten minutes before the service, I would sit in front of the sanctuary facing the congregation and give anyone who wanted me to pray with and for them an opportunity to come to the front row pew for prayer. I then took their hands and asked for their prayer request and prayed with them.

On the last Sunday of the month and during the Maundy Thursday Service, we had a time for prayer and healing for any individual or other people by request. I had them come to the front row pew. Then one at a time, I had them either kneel at a kneeler or sit in a chair. I would place my hands on their head if kneeling, and take their hands if seated and ask for their request. Then with the Deacons or Board Members standing behind them placing their hands on their shoulders, I asked the congregation to pray silently for their request. Then I prayed aloud for them.

I would like to share two prayers my Dad gave me many years ago. I pray these prayers with individuals and give the written prayers to them so that they can pray for themselves. The following prayer I pray everyday for myself and with others.

### A Personal Prayer for Health

Our loving Heavenly Father, I thank you for all of the wonderful things you are doing for me. (Thank God for specific things past and present that God has done for you.)

Forgive me for all my mistakes and my sins. (Ask for forgiveness for specific sins and mistakes of the past. Visualize Jesus placing his hands on your head and saying that you are forgiven.) Help me to forgive myself and others. Thank you Lord Jesus. Holy Spirit come into my body. Send your healing power down through my head, neck, shoulders, arms, body, and legs like a stream of living water flowing through my entire body. Send your healing power into every muscle, every nerve, and every cell of my body destroying all germs, viruses and diseases. Send your healing power into (a specific area where you need healing) and heal (that area.)

(If a disease, visualize thousands of white corpuscles attacking the diseased cells and devouring these cells like "Pac-Man" and then sweeping back through your body devouring any stray germs.)

(If an operation or broken bone, visualize the healing taking place with the tissues and bones coming together and mending.)

(Then pray) Heal me. Thank you, Holy Spirit. Thank you, Lord Jesus. Thank you, Heavenly Father.

Lord Jesus, send your healing light into my mind, and clean out all negative and evil thoughts. Help me to think positive thoughts, good thoughts, happy thoughts. Thank you, Lord Jesus.

Heavenly Father, calm my nerves and emotions. Take away all worry, anxiety and fear. Help me to know that you are with me every minute of every day and that I don't need to worry because you are taking care of me. Help me to know that you are surrounding me and protecting me all of the time especially when I sleep. Give me a good day and a good night's sleep and help me to wake refreshed, ready for a new day tomorrow. Help me all day today, and bless me.

(Then offer any prayers you may have for others and end your prayer with) In Jesus' Name, Amen.

## *A Relaxation Prayer for Stress and Health*

This second prayer my Dad, a pastor for 63 years, gave me before he went on to Glory. I pray this prayer with people who have the time, and I suggest that they read it for themselves, or have someone else read it as they relax.

Get comfortable in a chair or lying in bed.

Begin praying visualizing each step as you pray.

Heavenly Father, release and relax all of the muscles and nerves up and down my back bone. Release and relax the muscles in the top of my head. Release and relax the muscles and nerves in my brain. Release and relax the muscles in my forehead. (Imagine your forehead sinking into you head.)

Dear Lord, release and relax all of the muscles in my eyes, my nose, my mouth, my chin, (let your mouth fall open). Dear Lord release and relax all of the muscles in my neck. (Twist your neck gently to the right and to the left.) Dear Lord, release and relax all of the muscles in my shoulders, down my left arm, my biceps, my elbow, my forearm, my wrist, my hand, my fingers. Dear Lord, release and relax all of the muscles down my right arm, my biceps, my elbow, my forearm, my wrist, my hand, my fingers.

Dear Lord, release and relax the muscles in my chest, my lungs, my heart, my stomach, my large intestines, my small intestines, all of my internal organs, my pelvic area, my hips, the small of my back. Dear Lord, release and relax the muscles down my left leg, my thigh, my knee, my calf, my ankle, my foot, my toes. Dear Lord, release and relax all of the muscles down my right leg, my thigh, my knee, my calf, my ankle, my foot, my toes. Dear Lord, release and relax all of the muscles in my entire body.

(Say out loud) Heavenly Father I love you. Jesus I love you. Holy Spirit I love you. (Confess any bitterness or sins and ask forgiveness. Imagine Jesus putting his hand on your head and saying, "I forgive you. Go and sin no more.")

(Then pray) Heavenly Father, send your healing power into my body beginning at the top of my head and continuing down through my head, throat, arms, body, and legs like a warm neon light healing my entire body. (If you have a specific area of your body that is hurting, visualize that warm healing presence of God healing that area.)

(Then ask God to send his healing light into your mind to clean out all negative and evil thoughts. Follow this by asking God to send his healing light into your nerves and emotions calming and quieting them.)

(Pray) Thank you Heavenly Father. Thank you Lord Jesus. Thank you Holy Spirit.

(Visualize Jesus standing before you with his arms extended in front of him waiting to take your problems. Visualize Jesus taking your problems one by one. Pray.) Thank you, Jesus. Amen.

Realize that Jesus has your problems and he will take care of them for you. You will continue to feel relaxed. Now go off to sleep knowing that everything will be all right. Sleep soundly trusting Jesus completely.

Wake up refreshed knowing God is with you and He will help you through another day.

Another effective way of praying this prayer is to have another person pray it aloud with you, guiding your thoughts.

## *Suggestions for a Hospital Ministry*

I was a hospital chaplain in the largest Air Force hospital for three years, and I'd like to share what I learned from my experience.

When a person is admitted to a hospital, usually they are filled with anxiety and fear because they are in a foreign environment and don't know what will happen to them.

It is important that a pastor make contact with the person on the day before the member enters the hospital and that he or she prays with the member focusing on the assurance that God is with them and the doctors and the nurses and asking for God's presence in their lives and in the hospital room. It is important to pray that God's presence be with the person at all times. Tell the member that you, and all the members of the church will be praying for them. Then assure the member that you will visit them after their procedure.

This first contact may be in the person's home or if you are busy make the contact and pray with them on the phone. If the patient is going to be observed for several days before an operation, I make sure that I visit or call the patient on the day before the operation and pray with them.

When the patient's operation is completed and he or she is ready, I phone them and pray with them.

When I visit anyone in the hospital the first thing I do is to wash my hands. As a hospital chaplain I washed my hands all day long after visiting every patient.

If you are on a limited time schedule do not sit down in the patient's room. Remain standing and talk and pray with the patient. It is easier to say you have to leave for some reason in this way.

I try not to share anything of a negative nature that may upset the patient. Concentrate on the positives.

Assure the patient that they are in a fine hospital and that the doctors and nurses are dedicated people.

Tell the patient that they are looking good, and that everyone in the church is praying for them. Try to pose questions that will get positive answers like, *"How are the nurses and doctors treating you?" "It's good to have a hospital when we need it."* Ask how they are feeling. They will probably tell you all about their operation. When it is a tragic situation, say, *"At a time like this we feel so helpless. No one knows why; but God is with us and God will help us."* Relate positive things about the church and bring them a bulletin or newsletter. If possible share some humor with the patient.

When I visit terminal patients or patients confined to a bed or chair, I get them to talk about the happy days when they were children by asking them about their childhood days. Get them to talk about their favorite teacher, birthday, or subjects in school. When I was a hospital chaplain, one terminally ill lady said, *"I look forward to your visits because after you leave I recall happy memories of when I was young for three or four hours and it makes the time go by."* This could help any patient.

Before I leave, I always take their hands and pray for their healing and for the doctors and nurses and their loved ones. If they are up to it, we pray the Lord's Prayer together. This gives them an opportunity to be a part of the prayer. I leave a copy of one of the prayers I have shared with you.

I always wash my hands after leaving a patient to see another patient or if I am going somewhere else.

If I am making a house call, I always phone before I visit them as sometimes it is not convenient for you to visit.

If I have a busy schedule and I find that I cannot visit someone, I make a telephone call and tell them I'm sorry that I cannot visit them and then suggest that we have a prayer over the telephone. This is usually welcomed by the person.

The most important thing in visiting a person is to show them that you care. Your presence will be more comforting to them than anything you may say.

# Chapter Nineteen

## *Getting a Church off of a Plateau*

One of the most difficult things that any pastor has to cope with in his or her ministry is changing the members' mentality from complacency to active involvement in evangelism and church growth. When complacency moves in, the church members are satisfied with everything the way it is and they are not interested in reaching others with the Gospel.

After ten years, like any church, our members became comfortable and satisfied with their church programs and activities and they weren't interested in reaching other people for the Lord. The Church Board decided to celebrate a "Bring a Friend Sunday" with a two month lead time to focus everyone's attention on outreach.

I began the process of getting the members off the plateau by preaching a sermon on "Power Praying." I used Luke 11:9 as the Scripture for my message. In this passage Jesus says *"Ask and you will receive; seek and you will find; knock and the door will be opened unto you."* Then I re-stated these promises with, "ask and you might receive;"

"seek and maybe you will find;" "knock and the door might be opened." Jesus did not say might or maybe but he gave us a positive message that it would happen.

Power Praying will make it happen. Then I illustrated it with proven prayer experiments and Jesus' answer to why the disciples couldn't heal a child. (Matthew 17:14-21) I stated that we as a church seem to have hit a plateau, like all churches from time to time. I stated that we were pretty satisfied with our church the way it is but that is not what Jesus taught his disciples and us. We need to earnestly pray and ask God to help and guide us, not just for a couple of minutes a day, but for longer periods. I suggested that <u>Wednesdays be Power Praying Days</u> for the next two months. I placed an insert in the bulletin with the following suggestions:

*"Every Wednesday between now and '<u>Bring A Friend Sunday</u>,' let's pray for specific individuals that need the Lord and our church programs and activities. This can be done anytime of the day in our homes, or at work, or at a Silent Prayer Retreat in the Church Sanctuary from 10:00 a.m. to noon. People can come and go as they please. Suggested prayers and meditations would be available at the entrance of the sanctuary. If you like, I will pray with you for specific requests during the Silent Prayer Retreat."*

It is suggested that each of us pray especially for one or two individuals who need our Lord. Ask the Lord to come into the person's life, and visualize the person meeting our Lord, and enjoying His company. Let the Lord help the person. See how the person reacts, and ask a blessing for the person. Then ask the person to come to church with you. If you are uncomfortable asking them, do it when we celebrate "<u>Bring A Friend Sunday</u>," and explain that there will be others there that usually do not attend a Sunday Service. They will not be the only ones.

It is important that we each pray for the specific programs of our church. Ask the Lord to come into that program or activity and visualize the chosen activity with many happy people or children enjoying it. Let the Lord fill the activity with His love. Ask God to bless it.

I created a form for the bulletin preparing for the "Bring A Friend Sunday." This is the suggested form.

> Please fill in this form and place it in the offering plate as your commitment to God and our church. Do not write individual names, but do write the numbers of the programs or activities you will be praying for during your daily devotions. We want to make sure that someone is praying for all of the specific programs and activities.

### *Suggested Programs and Activities*

1. Beginners Class
2. Primary Class
3. Junior Class
4. Jr. High Class
5. Sr. High Class
6. Sunday Adult Class
7. Tuesday Adult Bible Class
8. Monday Prayer Group
9. A Parenting Course (begins in the fall)
10. Lydia Circle
11. Men's Breakfast Group
12. Sunday Worship Service
13. DIAL HOPE Telephone Outreach Ministry
14. The Board Members
15. The Deacons

16. The Pastor
I will be praying for at least one individual who needs Our Lord.

I will pray Wednesdays for programs or activities (numbers 1-16). _____

Signed_____

I ended the sermon with, *"We all want our church to grow and reach others for our Lord. Jesus challenged his disciples to pray for themselves and others. Let's do it. Let's begin by dedicating or rededicating our lives to God during a time of silent prayer. Just pray, 'Heavenly Father, come into my life, and help me to reach others for you. In Jesus' Name. Amen.'"*

The "Bring a Friend Sunday," included beginning a Parenting Video Course or a Marriage Enrichment Course during the Sunday School hour so the children could attend a Sunday School class at the same time. It is important to plan for a church newsletter and distribution of flyers to the entire community just before the "Bring A Friend Sunday." Put a news release in the newspapers and announcements on radio.

Beginning a new outreach ministry and getting the Church Board's approval is always a way to create enthusiasm in the members for the church's mission. This will also provide a public relations opportunity to show the community an additional facet of the church's image. In addition to video/DVD courses to help people in the community, tutoring grade school students one afternoon a week or volunteering to visit troubled youths in the juvenile hall or other ways of helping people in the community will enrich the members' lives and the life of the church.

Doing all of these things will help any church off of their plateau but prayer is the most important force. Prayer is the most powerful force in our world today.

*Never underestimate the power of God.*

# Appendix

## *The How to Do It Dial Hope Manual*

The DIAL HOPE Telephone Outreach Ministry is a proven, simple, inexpensive, minimum effort, non threatening way to reach the unchurched. A caller hears a Scripture, a thought for the day, a prayer, and an invitation to request prayer and come to a Sunday Service, twenty-four hours a day, seven days a week with a recorded telephone message, changed daily except Saturdays and holidays. The development and results of the DIAL HOPE Telephone Outreach Ministry can be found in Chapter Fourteen of this book. This Manual explains how to set it up.

### *Equipment and Its Use*

When the DIAL HOPE Ministry began in the 1990s, all of the telephone answering machines had two microcassettes, one for the message and the other for the prayer requests. A pastor would record his message on a microcassette and change the microcassette each day. The caller's prayer request would automatically be recorded on the other cassette.

Slowly every corporation making telephone answering machines began changing from microcassettes to digital answering machines. Only the TAKACAM Manufacturing Company kept manufacturing commercial microcassette answering machines but they discontinued their production of making cassette machines for digital machines in 2005.

Today all corporations making telephone answering machines are digital with about thirty seconds for messages, and up to three minutes for an answer.

The daily DIAL HOPE Scripture, message, prayer and invitation to attend Sunday Services take about six minutes.

I have found an answer to this dilemma; a commercial heavy duty Message Announcer Machine that will provide six minutes for a DIAL HOPE message.

The 1200 ELR Digital Announcer Machine manufactured by RACOM Products Incorporated comes with five or six minute message times. It only carries an announcement. It does not have the ability to record an answer by the listener.

To use the 1200 ELR Machine it is necessary to record the complete DIAL HOPE message and prayer on a cassette recorder with a tape counter indicator to know where one devotional ends and the new devotional begins. Then the DIAL HOPE message is downloaded each day into the 1200 ELR machine.

There are at least two cassette recorder machines with tape counters that can be purchased at Office Depot for about $35.00. They are Sony: M-570 and Olympus: J-300.

The 1200 ELR Announcer can be purchased from RACOM Products Incorporation by calling (800) 722.6664

or WWW.RACOMINC.COM for $460.00 (Churches

10% discount) It is also important to buy a cable to download the recorded devotional from the cassette recorder to the <u>1200 ELR Announcer</u> for $15.00. If you want to count the number of calls, a machine to be added to the 1200 ELR, is $95.00.

Another dealer for the 1200 ELR Announcer in Los Angeles is <u>TEMAR COMMUNICATIONS</u> (800) 750.9050 or <u>WWW.TEMAR.NET</u>). He gives a discount to churches.

I suggest that as you record the daily devotionals on the cassette recorder, note the tape counter number at the end of each devotional so that you know where to begin the next day's devotional. After recording the day's devotion, put the recorder on play and count to ten. This will space the devotionals. Each day the devotional will be downloaded into the announcing machine. Listen to the machine in the Announcer. It will automatically return to the beginning of the devotional when finished.

For prayer requests, it will be necessary to include at the end of the DIAL HOPE devotional an invitation to call a different phone number for a person to leave a recorded prayer request. I suggest you ask the caller to leave a phone number so that you can follow up to help them.

To fund the Dial Hope Ministry, some churches use their Memorial Fund, or they dedicate the DIAL HOPE Ministry to a member who contributes the funds for the Dial Hope machines and the phone lines to the church.

### *Preparing the Devotional*

Before beginning to record the devotional on the cassette recorder, take a notebook and list the number of the tape counter of the recorder and designate the devotional in some way. When you complete the devotional, record the number on the counter of the recorder. (Continue this process for each devotional.) Then you will be able to find it if necessary and you will know how to download it to the announcement machine.

## Preparing the Scripture Reading

For meaningful Scriptures I use several verses from the Psalms. The Psalms often speak directly to the needs of individuals, like Psalm 34. I select only the verses that speak to a person's needs and then I underline them to make it easier to read. I don't necessarily try to match the Scripture with the thought for the day. The caller may receive help from either the Scripture or the thought for the day.

For help in selecting verses in the Psalms, you might take a Bible to a shut-in and have them select and highlight or underline only the verses that speak directly to their needs. Then the person recording the devotional can read those special verses. You could give credit to the person who selects the verses.

## The Thought for the Day

Since all daily devotional booklets are copyrighted, it is necessary to receive permission from the publisher by sending a letter, fax or calling them on the phone. I think your denominational daily devotionals would be happy to have you use their devotions without copyright. You might obtain back issues of the devotionals by contacting the publisher or by asking the members of your church for back issues. I knew one lady who kept the devotionals for years.

It is important to credit both the publisher and the writer before you read the thought for the day. Do not use their material for profit or gain.

After selecting your devotional material, I suggest that you carry it in your pocket when you know you are going to have to wait somewhere, such as in a barber shop or a doctor's office. I read the daily thoughts for the day selecting those that would be of interest to the callers. I try to select those that are not "preachy" because I know that the majority of the callers are usually not related to a church.

When I find a devotional that would interest the caller, I write "Good" at the top of the page, if not I write "No." This makes it easier to select when I record. I number the devotional at the top of the page and put the number on the list in the notebook when you record it.

Immediately before recording, I mark the thought for the day by underlining the end of the second line, and the beginning of the third line, continuing to underline at the beginning of every other line of the paragraphs. This makes it easier to read and eliminates reading errors.

As I read through the thought I underline difficult words to make sure of my pronunciation.

### *Suggestions for Extemporaneous Prayers*

I use the short prayer at the end of the devotional for the beginning of the extemporaneous prayer.

I make a general list of people (not specific individuals) to pray for who are: lonely, anxious, worried, facing severe problems, in pain, needing forgiveness, mourning lost loved ones, facing temptations, fearful, suffering from accidents, operations, in need of healing, coping with alcoholism, drugs, temptations, over eating, etc.

Then I pick out one of these subjects to pray for that day. The prayer subject doesn't necessarily need to correspond with the thought for the day.

I never pray for a person by name since I do not know when the devotional will be scheduled and should I want to repeat it in a year, it would be dated.

I never refer to the time of day when I am taping the prayer like morning, afternoon or evening. I always refer to "day," like "Lord, bless us today." Many people call in at night and if they hear references to morning they will not feel the immediacy of the prayer.

I always end the extemporaneous prayer by saying, *"Heavenly Father, come with power, into our lives. Heal us and help us with our problems, we pray. Thank you for healing and helping us. In Jesus' Name, Amen."*

### Recording the Devotional

It will take two or three hours twice a month to actually record the DIAL HOPE tapes for the month. Set aside two hours you can record without interruption in a place with a minimum amount of noise. Turn off the phone.

Do not worry about outside noises like cars going by or airplanes going by overhead. The microphone installed in the recording machine will not pick up these noises. The only sound that I record around is the town clock striking the hour. When I first began recording, I let the outside noises bother me and it was a real trial. After a time I realized that the outside noises made no difference and it made recording a lot easier. The microphone built into the machine will pick up your voice at a table in your home or desk in the office.

*Do not try to be perfect!* At first I tried to record flawlessly like a radio announcer. It was a real trial by fire. I was in agony. Then I began to realize that I did not speak perfectly and that no one does. I relaxed and did my best. I actually believe people listen more intently and hear better when we aren't perfect. So relax. Do your best and let God bless your message and prayer.

Keep all devotionals for future use. They can be used during your annual vacation, when you get in a bind, and after a year or two you can use them over again.

## Day-to-Day Operation

After completing the taping for a week or two, I take a calendar and put the tape counter numbers of the devotionals on the cassette tape in the day's square. The person who downloads the tape recording on a specific day, initials the square.

Downloading the tape is the first priority of the work day. Tapes are not changed on Saturdays, Sundays or holidays.

The person who downloads the devotional, then checks the prayer requests phoned to the special prayer request phone number and gives them to the pastor. The names and requests are included during the Sunday Service Silent Prayer time and included in the prayer requests on the back of the Sunday bulletin.

After downloading the devotional, phone the DIAL HOPE number to be sure the machine is functioning properly.

## Security of the Machine

When you have a telephone line installed in the church for DIAL HOPE, I suggest that the line run into the pastor's office for privacy and security. It could be installed behind a cabinet so the announcing machine can be placed in the cabinet out of sight. We had two machines stolen in the church office. We think someone saw the machines while visiting the office.

## *Publicity*

Without an on-going publicity program, the DIAL HOPE Ministry will not reach the people who need it.

Use newspaper news releases, feature stories and free ads in weekly newspapers to keep DIAL HOPE in the minds of the people. Keeping a want ad in a free weekly newspaper is a good idea because often people may not need DIAL HOPE one week, but would welcome it the next week. Below is an example of a twenty-five word ad:

WANT A SPIRITUAL LIFT? Call DIAL HOPE (put the phone number here) recording changed daily.

FOR AN INFORMAL SUNDAY SERVICE 10:00 a.m. All are Welcome! (The name and address of the church)

DIAL HOPE Business Cards can be used by the members, to be given to others as their personal evangelism effort. Be sure that the first line is a "Hook." Our business cards read:

"Would you like a spiritual lift?"

DIAL HOPE (Phone number) 24 hour recording changed daily, by The Friendly Caring People of (Name of church)

Sunday Worship Services 10:00 a.m.

(Name and address of Church) Office (phone number)
EVERYONE WELCOME!

DIAL HOPE can be included in church flyers, placed in local newspapers, or distributed by the Boy Scouts to each house.

For writing ads and brochures, use the same advice as writing news releases and articles. (See writing News Releases and Articles for Newspapers in Chapter 13.)

## *Suggested DIAL HOPE Scripts*

Opening comments need to make first time callers feel welcome. I have used the following script for the past ten years. It seems to be successful. Use it as it is or as a guide.

Hello, this is _____. I'm happy (I change it often to "really glad") you called. I hope you will find something in the Scripture, the thought for the day, or the prayer that can give you a spiritual lift, and help you with the living of your life.

Our scripture today is selected verses from the Psalms. I am reading from (the translation of the Bible). Read the Scripture. Following the Scripture reading, state the book and chapter. (Reading the book and chapter before the Scripture reading might lose the unchurched caller.)

Our thought for the day comes to us from (Name of devotional) and (writer's name) He/she writes (read devotional).

Let's come to God in Prayer. (Extemporaneous prayer) I always end my prayer with: Heavenly Father, come with power into our lives.

Heal us and help us with our problems, we pray. Thank you for healing and helping us. In Jesus' name. Amen."

The DIAL HOPE meditations are brought to you by the friendly caring people of the (Church). Our church is located at (address)

The DIAL HOPE meditations are changed every morning between nine and ten o'clock except on Saturdays, Sundays and holidays.

I believe in the power of prayer. If you would like to have me pray for you, or if someone you know needs prayer, just call our prayer request number (_____).I will pray for you and your request during my morning devotions. The prayer request phone number is _____.

'More things are wrought through prayer than this world dreams of.'

We would like to invite you to worship with us at _____ o'clock on Sunday mornings. We have a warm friendly service that I know you will enjoy. I don't know about you, but when I visit a church, I don't like to have to stand up and introduce myself. You will never have to do this in our services. If you have never attended a church service, everyone is given an order of worship as they arrive. Then it is a simple matter to follow the order of worship. We hope you will worship with us next Sunday at _____ o'clock. We hope you will call again tomorrow. Tell your friends and neighbors about DIAL HOPE. Perhaps it will help them, too. This is _____. May God bless you and your loved ones today.

This is only a suggested script. Modify it to your needs.

## Suggested News Release

A news release should be brief and to the point so the editor, who gets a huge volume of news releases everyday, can see the facts immediately. If he or she wants more details he or she will call you. Double space all news releases. Type the news release and copy it on your church stationery.

Date:

Your name and phone number.

NEWS RELEASE:

DIAL HOPE TELEPHONE PROGRAM BEGINS

A new daily recorded DIAL HOPE Telephone Program, (telephone number with area code), will begin on (date) for anyone who wants a spiritual lift.

A caller will hear a recorded Scripture, a thought for the day and a prayer, with an opportunity to request prayer by calling a prayer request number.

The prayer request number is _____. The pastor and others will pray for you.

The twenty-four hour recorded devotional will be changed everyday between 9:00 a.m. and 10:00 a.m. except for Saturdays, Sundays and holidays.

The (name and address of your church) is sponsoring the DIAL HOPE Program. For more information, phone the church office (phone number.)

## A Junior Member Basic Christian Beliefs Course

This course is written in the vocabulary of the junior student and is to be used as a guide for teaching juniors.

The teacher should help the students understand difficult words and concepts. It is suggested that lessons be copied and given to the students for their notebooks to take home for future reference.

Who Is God?

Have you ever planted a flower seed, and watched it grow?

First there is a green blade. Then it changes from a green plant to a bud, and then to a beautiful flower with bright colors.

How did it happen?

Have you ever seen a baby bird in a nest? At first all the baby bird does is eat what the mother bird brings to it. Then it gets bigger and it can walk. Finally it stretches its wings and flies.

How does this happen?

All around us we see things happen. After the winter, the sun warms the earth and everything starts growing. The trees with bare branches sprout green leaves. The plants start growing and the world is beautiful.

What makes all of this happen?

Thousands of years ago, some people saw all of these things happening. They thought that something must have made all these things. They called this something, "God."

They asked God to speak to them. Then they wrote what God told them. We have their thoughts in the Bible.

In the first verse in the Bible we read, "In the beginning, God created the heavens and the earth. (Genesis 1:1)

Then we read how God created the world and everything in it.

It tells us what God did each day. When you see the word day in the Bible it often means more than one day. It could mean that a day could have been a thousand years or more. (Read Psalm 90:4.)

To see how God created the world, begin by reading the first twenty seven verses in the Bible. As you read them fill in the blanks.

What Did God Do Each Day?

FIRST DAY

_____

SECOND DAY

_____

THIRD DAY

_____

FOURTH DAY

_____

FIFTH DAY

_____

SIXTH DAY

_____

SEVENTH DAY

_____

God created our world and us. But God is more than just our creator. God is our Heavenly Father. (Isaiah 64:8; Matthew 6:9)

God loves you and me.

As we read the Bible, we find that the writers tell us that God loves us. God wants to help us to live happy lives.

In the Old Testament, in about the middle of the Bible you find the Psalms. Many of the writers of the Book of

Psalms tell us that God helped them and that God will help us.

God helps us when we feel sorry for ourselves. (Psalm 34)

God helps us when we are afraid. (Psalm 46)

God helps us when we are sick. (Psalm 30)

God helps us when we are sad. When someone dies God comforts us. (Psalm 23)

God helps us to know how to live happy lives. (Psalm 1)

*From Psalm 34 in the King James Bible, fill in the blanks with the correct answers: (KJV)*

Verse 4 (The Lord) delivered me from all my ___ ___ ___ ___

Verse 6 The Lord heard him and saved him out of all his ___ ___ ___ ___ ___ ___ ___ ___.

Verse 13 Keep Thy ___ ___ ___ ___ ___ ___ from evil, and thy ___ ___ ___ ___ from speaking guile.

Verse 14 and do ___ ___ ___ ___ Seek ___ ___ ___ ___ ___ and pursue it.

PSALM 23

Verse 1 The Lord is my ___ ___ ___ ___ ___ ___ ___ ___.

Verse 2 He maketh me to lie down in green ___ ___ ___ ___ ___ ___ ___ ___.

Verse 3 He restoreth my ___ ___ ___ ___.

Verse 4 I will fear no ___ ___ ___ ___.

Verse 6 I will dwell in the ___ ___ ___ ___ ___ of The Lord forever.

In the New Testament, Jesus came to show us what God is like. He tells us what God wants us to do to live happy lives. (John 10:10)

Jesus says many times that God is our Heavenly Father. (Matthew 6:9)

In the parable, or story, of the Prodigal Son (Luke 15:11-32) Jesus shows us that God loves us just as we are. God forgives us. God wants to help us. But like the prodigal son, we have to come to Him.

There are many more verses in the Psalms and in the New Testament that can help us. That is why it is good to read a page a day in the Psalms and Matthew.

Many years before Jesus was born, people were different. They were cruel to each other. They were not happy.

God loved them.

God gave them laws or rules to help them live happy lives.

The people often broke the laws. They would not do what God wanted them to do. Then God punished them to help them. They thought God was mean.

God wanted to show them that He loved them. He sent Jesus, His son, to show people what He was really like.

When we read about Jesus and his life and teachings, we see what God is really like. Jesus said that God is our Heavenly Father. He loves us and wants to help us to live happy lives.

Think of the most wonderful earthly father you can think of; a father who loves his children, a father who will do anything he can to help his children, a father who will not hurt his children.

Jesus says God is like that father, only God is even more loving, and kind, and helpful than any earthly father.

God will always love, and help you, when you ask Him to come into your life and help you.

## *God Is the Son*

Do you like birds?

Have you ever seen a farm with all the fields of crops growing?

Have you ever visited a zoo and seen foxes?

Many years ago when Jesus was a boy he liked birds. He visited farmers and saw how crops grew. He also knew about foxes and probably about other kinds of animals, too.

Do you know how we know that Jesus knew all about these things? It is because later in His life when He taught people about God. He talked about birds, seeds, and foxes.

Jesus was a boy just like boys today. He played with His brothers and sisters. (Matthew 13:55, 56)

His father was a carpenter, and He learned to be a carpenter too.

We know that Jesus lived in Nazareth with His mother, Mary, and His earthly father, Joseph.

We know that Jesus went to school in the synagogue which is like a church today. We know He memorized verses from the Old Testament because He often quoted verses from it when He taught people about God.

When He was twelve years old, His parents took Him to the temple in Jerusalem to celebrate His becoming a man.

Jesus always wanted to know many things. While He was at the temple, He asked the priests and teachers many questions about God.

The temple leaders were surprised at His questions. They liked to talk with Jesus. He liked talking with them so much that He forgot to go with His parents when they left the temple to start walking home to Nazareth.

Mary walked with the women and Joseph walked with

the men. Each one thought that Jesus was with the other person. They walked all day. Then they tried to find Jesus. He wasn't with anyone. They hurried back to Jerusalem to find Jesus.

They finally found Him in the temple with the leaders of the temple. They asked Him why He had stayed behind. Jesus said, "I must be about my Father's business," (Luke 2:49 KJV).

They were happy to find Him, and took Him home with them to Nazareth. Jesus grew to be a strong, young man.

*Read the verse listed and fill in the blanks with the correct answers:*

Matthew 13:55. What are the names of the brothers of Jesus? _____, _____, _____, _____.

Luke 9:58 Jesus said, "Foxes have _____, Birds have _____, The Son of Man has no _____.

Luke 12:6,&7 What birds did Jesus talk about? _____.

John 12:24 What kind of farm plant did Jesus talk about? _____.

People wonder what Jesus meant when He said, "I must be about my Father's business."

Before Jesus was born, His mother, Mary, was engaged to marry Joseph.

An angel came to Mary and told her not to be afraid. God was going to give her a son. She was to call him Jesus. She was told, "He will be great and will be called the Son of God." (Luke 1:26-33)

Jesus was born in Bethlehem.

The shepherds heard the angels say that Jesus would be born in Bethlehem, so they went to see him.

The wise men saw a star in the east and came to worship Jesus.

This is why Jesus said, "I must be about my Father's business." He was the Son of God.

We don't know what happened to Jesus between the ages of twelve and thirty. The men who wrote about his life in the Bible did not think it was important.

When he was thirty years old, he went to hear John the Baptist preach by the Jordan River. John the Baptist baptized Jesus. Jesus heard the voice of God say that He was His Son. He knew that His purpose in life was to help people know what God was like.

After His baptism, Jesus went into the wilderness alone. He prayed and went without food for forty days.

While He was in the desert, He was tempted by the devil to break the commandments of God. The devil said he knew an easy way to get people to follow him.

The devil told Him to make bread out of stones to feed the people. Then the people would follow Him. Jesus knew that this was the wrong reason to follow God.

The devil took Him to a high tower and told Him to jump off. The devil said that God would not let Him hurt Himself. Jesus knew that people would not follow God because He did something dangerous.

The devil took Him to a high mountain. Jesus could see for miles. The devil said, "Kneel down and worship me and I will give you all the people on the earth." Jesus knew that if He worshiped the devil He could not do God's will. He told the devil to get away from Him.

Then the devil left Him.

God sent angels to teach Him. The angels taught Jesus how to reach people for God.

Then Jesus chose twelve men. He taught them about

God for three years.

As He was teaching them, He was also teaching hundreds of other people who came to listen to Him. Jesus healed people and did many miracles to help people to know God.

The religious leaders of His day didn't like Jesus. They saw that many people were following Jesus and not them. They decided to kill Jesus. They thought the crowds of people who followed Jesus would come back to follow them if Jesus was dead.

Jesus knew they would try to kill Him. Jesus also knew that if He died on a cross, He could save people from their sins. He could give them a new life with God.

Jesus went to Jerusalem where the religious leaders lived. The religious leaders crucified Jesus. Jesus died on a cross.

A friend of Jesus put His body in his tomb.

Three days later, in the morning, ladies came to the tomb. Jesus was not there.

He had risen! Jesus was alive!

Jesus visited His disciples. They saw that He was alive. He was not like them because He could walk through doors. He would vanish and appear miles away.

Then His disciples knew that Jesus would be with them and help them wherever they were. Jesus told the disciples to go to everyone in the world. He told them to do what God wanted them to do.

He told them that when anyone dedicated their life to God and said they would follow His teachings, the disciples were to baptize them. He told them to continue to teach them what He had taught them during the three years He taught them.

Jesus said, "I will be with you always to help you and guide you."

The disciples began preaching and teaching what Jesus had taught them. Many people believed them and followed the teachings of Jesus. Then these people told others and the others told others, until someone told you, and someone told me. Now it is our turn to tell others about Jesus and what God is really like.

Jesus, God's Son, came down to our earth from heaven to show us what God is like. He came to save us from our sins. When we follow Jesus, we will read our Bibles, go to Sunday School and Worship Services and pray.

God will help us to have a wonderful life.

We can read about Jesus, and his life and teachings, in the Books of Matthew, Mark, Luke, and John in the New Testament. Read one page a day and you will get to know God and Jesus better.

### *God Is the Holy Spirit*

Have you ever watched the wind blow through the trees?

Have you ever been alone, and thought your mother or father was with you?

Have you ever wanted to do something wrong and you thought you shouldn't do it?

Have you ever wanted something and decided to work to get it?

The Holy Spirit is like the wind. You can feel it but you do not know where it comes from or where it is going.

When you feel that your mother or father is with you when you are alone, the Holy Spirit is like that.

The Holy Spirit is like your thoughts when you do what is right.

When you decide to do something good for yourself,

the Holy Spirit will be guiding you if you ask for His help.

God is our Creator Father, our Savior Jesus Christ and the Holy Spirit.

No one can see the Holy Spirit, but the Holy Spirit is in the world and the Holy Spirit helps us and guides us when we ask for help.

Jesus told his disciples when he went to heaven that he would leave the Holy Spirit to comfort and help and guide them. (John 14:15-31)

God is the Creator Father, the Son Jesus Christ, and the Holy Spirit. It is not easy to understand that God is the Father, Son, and Holy Spirit. One simple way to explain this is that God is like a man.

A man is a father to his son. He is a son to his parents. He is a husband to his wife. He is one person but three different persons at the same time. But God is much more than this in many ways.

God is so great that we will never know all there is to know about God. As we live our lives we will keep finding out more and more about God. We will come to know God better and better.

Remember, God is our loving Heavenly Father. He wants to help us have a happy life. He will always help us when we ask for his help.

Jesus shows us what God is like.

The Holy Spirit is with us in our thoughts all the time. The Holy Spirit guides us, and helps us do the right thing. He gives us the strength to do it.

The Holy Spirit comforts us when we feel alone, or when we lose someone in our family, or a friend.

We can understand that God is the Father, Son, and Holy Spirit by asking God, in prayer, to help us.

We can learn about God by reading about Him in the

Bible. We can know Him by going to Sunday School and Sunday Worship Services every week.

God loves you now, and He will always love you, no matter what you do. God will always forgive you when you ask to be forgiven.

God wants to be your friend for life.

Be a friend to God, and He will help you all through your life.

### The Bible

When you read a good book, what do you like?

Do you like adventure stories?

Do you like mysteries?

Do you like to read about people?

Do you like to read about how people lived a long time ago?

Do you like to learn about something that will help you?

The Bible is filled with stories about people, adventures, mysteries and how people lived a long time ago, and how you can do things that will help you find happiness and a lot more.

The Bible is not just one book. The Bible has 66 books. They are all different, but the Bible has only one purpose. All 66 books in The Bible tell us about God and how God loves us and wants to help us.

### How Did We Get the Bible?

For many years, God inspired many writers to write things about our world and how we should live our lives. (2 Timothy 3:16) To be inspired means that God guided the thoughts of the writer.

One day a group of men who loved God, took all the books, the writers had written, and put them together in one book.

They called this book the Bible. The word "bible" comes from the Greek language and means "books." The Bible is a library of many books. It is known as The Scriptures or The Word of God.

The Bible is divided into two main sections; The Old Testament with 39 books and The New Testament with 27 books. The word testament means an agreement or promise between God and human beings. This agreement or promise is called a "covenant."

The Old Testament was written over 800 years, between 1200 and 200 B.C. The New Testament was written over about 50 years between 50 and 100 A.D.

The Old Testament was written in the Hebrew language. The New Testament was written in the Greek language.

All of the English-language Bibles have been translated from the Hebrew and Greek languages. That means that a word in the Hebrew or Greek language has been changed into an English word with the same meaning.

We learn about God, through true life adventures, mysteries, how people lived thousands of years ago, and the lives of men and women.

The Bible has one theme: that God loves all human beings and God wants to help them. The Bible tells us what God is like and how God works. God's plan for us is to help Him to help others.

It also tells us about God's love and God's power and God's goodness.

It tells us how we can find help in the living of our lives.

God gave everyone, "free will." This means that we are not robots. We can make choices. We can choose to do what we want to do. We can choose to do right or wrong.

God does not help us unless we choose to ask Him for help.

God loves all human beings, but God cannot help them unless they choose to ask Him.

## What Is in the Bible?

The Old Testament is about God's relationship with the Hebrew People.

In Genesis, we read about how God created the world. It tells us about how God chose Abraham to be the father of the Hebrew People.

God promised Abraham that if the Hebrew people followed Him, and did what He commanded, He would take care of them. If they chose not to follow Him, He would punish them.

## The Old Testament Has Many Kinds of Writings

### The Pentateuch

The first five books in the Bible are called the Pentateuch.

In the Book of Genesis, you will find out about the creation of the world and Adam and Eve. You will also learn about Abraham and the beginning of the Hebrew or Jewish people. You will read the story of Joseph and the coat of many colors and how the Hebrew People went to Egypt.

In the Book of Exodus, you will read about Moses and how the Hebrew People left Egypt and walked through the Red Sea on dry land, and how they wandered in the wilderness.

The Book of Leviticus is a book of laws.

In the Book of Numbers, the Hebrew People are in the wilderness and send spies into the Promised Land. The spies said they could not take the Promised Land. They kept wandering in the wilderness.

In the Book of Deuteronomy, the Hebrew People are waiting to go into the Promised Land. Moses speaks to the people and then he dies.

### The Books of History

In the Book of Joshua, you will read about how the Hebrew people enter the Promised Land. Joshua is the General of the Army. You will read about many battles.

The Book of Judges includes many stories about famous people. You will read about Gideon and Samson.

The Book of Ruth is a love story about a foreign woman who marries a Hebrew man. She becomes the great-grandmother of David.

The Books of First and Second Samuel begin when Samuel is a boy. His mother gives Samuel to God. He lives in the Temple and becomes a great judge. He anoints Saul and David, the first and second Hebrew Kings. (Anoint means he gives God's blessing to the two kings by putting olive oil on their heads.)

In the Books of First and Second Kings, you will read about David's death, and his son Solomon who becomes a king. Solomon builds a beautiful Temple in Jerusalem. When Solomon dies, the Hebrew nation is divided into two kingdoms. The Kingdom of Judah is in the south. The Kingdom of Israel is in the north.

The First and Second Books of Chronicles reviews the history of the Hebrew People.

Israel, the Northern Kingdom is conquered, and the people are taken to Assyria as slaves.

Judah, the Southern Kingdom is conquered. The temple is destroyed. The people are taken to Babylon to be slaves.

In the Book of Ezra, some of the people in Babylon are freed to go back to Judah. They rebuild the Temple in Jerusalem.

In the Book of Nehemiah, more people return to Judah. They rebuild the walls around Jerusalem.

The Book of Esther is about a Jewish woman named Esther who has great courage. She could have been killed, but she saves all the Hebrew slaves from death in Babylon

*The Books of Poetry*

In the Book of Job, you will read about a good man who loses everything. It asks the question, "Why do good people suffer?"

Job loses all of his money.

He loses all of his property.

He loses all of his cattle.

He loses all of his daughters.

He loses all of his sons.

He only has his wife left.

He loses his health and gets very sick.

His neighbors say that God took away everything. They tell him to blame God.

Job says he will never blame God. He will always trust God.

In the end, God blesses Job. He gets back everything he lost and more.

In the Book of Psalms, you will read what other people think about God. It is a hymn book and a prayer book for the Jewish people.

Jesus often quoted from the Psalms. It has helped people for thousands of years and it helps people today. Read a page a day from the Psalms. It will help you.

The Book of Proverbs has many wise sayings. It can help you make right choices in your life.

The Book of Ecclesiastes is a book of thoughts. The writer says to work hard and enjoy the gifts of God.

The Book of the Song of Solomon is a series of love poems written by Solomon.

### The Prophets

The rest of the books of the Old Testament were written by, and about men called prophets. Prophets were called by God to be His messengers to the Hebrew people. The prophets warned the Hebrew people that they should follow God and His commandments, or they would be punished. Sometimes they would tell the people what would happen in the future if they didn't follow God.

The prophets are called either major or minor prophets. The Major Prophets are prophets that wrote longer books in the Bible. The Minor Prophets are prophets that wrote smaller books in the Bible.

### The Major Prophets

In the Book of Isaiah, we read about the coming of the Messiah, which is Jesus. Every Christmas we hear words written by Isaiah. (Isaiah 9:6 & 7)

In the Book of Jeremiah, Jeremiah warns the people to follow God. He gives them hope. God will give them a new covenant that will be in their hearts and minds. He wants them to have a personal faith in God.

There are five poems in the Book of Lamentations.

They are sad poems about the suffering of the Hebrew people. There is one hope and that is when the writer has faith in God. (Lamentations 3:21-27)

In the Book of Ezekiel, Ezekiel says that Jerusalem will be destroyed if they do not return to God. Then he says that God will give them a new heart and new worship.

The first part of the Book of Daniel is about the adventures of Daniel and the lion's den. The last part is about Daniel's visions of the future.

### *The Minor Prophets*

In the Book of Hosea, Hosea loves his wife even when she doesn't love him. This shows us how God loves His people even when they sin against Him.

In the Book of Joel, Joel tells the people to repent of their sins. His famous message is that God will pour out His Spirit on all of the people. (Joel 2:28-29)

The Book of Amos is about justice. His famous message is "Let justice run down like water and righteousness like a mighty stream." (Amos 5:24 NKJV)

The Book of Jonah has the story of Jonah and the fish (whale). The message is that God loves all people, not just the Hebrews.

In the Book of Micah, Micah wants justice for people and real faith in God. In the future he says, God will bless people, and give them peace.

The Book of Nahum is a poem about the Assyrians being captured. He says God is Lord of all nations.

The Book of Habakkuk asks the question, "How can God allow evil people to be successful?" He says to have faith in God. You can trust God. God will help you.

In the Book of Haggai, Haggai tells the people to build a new temple.

The Book of Zechariah, has eight visions. He sees the coming Messiah, (Jesus).

In the Book of Malachi, Malachi says the people should obey God. God will bless them.

## *The New Testament*

### *The Four Gospels*

The Four Gospels: Matthew, Mark, Luke, and John tell the story of the life and teachings of Jesus. The crucifixion and resurrection of Jesus is found in the last chapters of all of the Four Gospels.

The Book of Matthew tells how Jesus is the Messiah by quoting verses from the books of The Old Testament. You will find The Lord's Prayer (Matthew 6:9-13), and the Sermon on The Mount (Matthew Chapters 5-7), which is a summary of the teachings of Jesus.

The Book of Mark tells us that Jesus is a man of action. You will find Jesus saying, *"Let the little children come unto me."* (Mark 10:13-16)

The Book of Luke was written by a doctor named Luke. You will find in this book, the story of the Birth of Jesus (Luke Chapters 1 & 2), the parable of the Good Samaritan (Luke 10:25-37), the parable of the Prodigal Son, (Luke 15:11-32), and the story of Zacchaeus (Luke 19:1-10).

The Book of John has the most famous verse in The New Testament: *"For God so loved the world that He gave His only begotten Son, that whoever believes in Him should not perish but have everlasting life."* (John 3:16 NKJV) You will also find the story of The Good Shepherd (John 10:1-16) and the promise of the coming of the Holy Spirit, (John 16:5-15).

The Book of Acts tells how the Christian Church

began. It tells how people in other countries learn about Jesus and his teachings. You will find out about the coming of the Holy Spirit during Pentecost, (Acts 2:1-4) and the first time the followers of Jesus were called Christians at Antioch, in Asia Minor (Acts 11:26), It also tells how the Apostle Paul founded churches in Asia Minor & Europe.

### The Letters or Epistles

The Apostles wrote letters to help individuals and churches. These letters are often called the Epistles. Epistles in the Greek language means letters. The titles of the Epistles are often the name of a city; what the people who live in that city are called; the name of the person it is addressed to; or the name of the Apostle who wrote the letter. The Apostle Paul wrote 13 of the 21 letters in the New Testament.

The Letter to the Romans by Paul is known for the teaching: *"The just shall live by faith."* (Romans 5:1-5) and *"Nothing can separate us from the love of God."* (Romans 8:35-39)

The Apostle Paul's two letters of First and Second Corinthians are written to the Christians of the Church of Corinth in Greece.

First Corinthians is known for the teaching of The Lord's Supper (1 Corinthians 11:17-34); how to overcome Temptation (1 Corinthians 10:13 KJV); and the real meaning of love (1 Corinthians Chapter 13).

In Second Corinthians, we find what Paul had to go through to bring us the teachings of Jesus (2 Corinthians 11:22-28).

In Galatians written to the Churches in Galatia in Turkey, Paul writes that we live by faith. (Galatians 2:20)

In Ephesians, written to the Church of Ephesus, Paul tells us to put on the Armor of God to protect us (Ephesians 6:10-17).

Philippians, Paul's letter to the Church of Philippi, is a letter of love and joy. He says, *"Press on toward the goal for the prize of the upward call of God in Christ Jesus."* (Philippines 3:14 NKJV)

Colossians, Paul's letter to the Church of Colosse, states that whatever you do, do your best. (Colossians 3:23-24)

First and Second Thessalonians are Paul's letters to the Church of Thessalonica in Greece.

In First Thessalonians 4:11-12, Paul says we should live quiet lives, and mind our own business.

In Second Thessalonians 3:6-14, Paul says do not be lazy but do good.

First and Second Timothy, are two letters to a young man named Timothy. Paul gives advice about being a pastor. He says the love of money is the root of all evil, (1 Timothy 6:10). He says to be a worker, who is not ashamed of his work. (2 Timothy 2:15)

Titus is written to a helper on the Island of Crete. Paul tells Titus what to do and teach.

Philemon, a slave, is a short personal letter from Paul to a member of the Church at Colosse asking him to welcome Philemon.

The Letter to the Hebrews was written to a group of Christians to help them with their faith in God. It is famous for the definition of faith. (Hebrews 11:1)

James, a letter written by James, the brother of Jesus, is about the way to live a Christian life. It states that we should not just listen to the Word of God, but put it into practice. (James 1:22-24)

First and Second Peter are letters written by the Apostle Peter. First Peter 1:3-5 gives us living hope. Second Peter 1:3-8, tells us how we should live.

First, Second and Third John are written by the Apostle John.

First John 1:5-10 is famous for the teaching of forgiveness and walking in the light of God.

Second and Third John are the shortest books in the Bible, and are written to a dear lady and her children, telling them to love one another. They are also written to Gainus to warn him against false teaching.

The brief letter, Jude, written by another brother of Jesus, is known for its famous benediction. (Jude 24-25)

The Revelation, written by John, is a book that tells of the final victory of Jesus Christ over all evil in the world. It has many visions that are hard to understand. The most famous verses (Revelation 21:1-4), tell us about the New Heaven and the New Earth.

These are only a few thoughts about each Book in the Bible There is much more to learn as you read your Bible.

### *The Christian Church*

The Christian Church began with Jesus, and His Twelve Disciples. "Disciple" means learner or student. The Twelve Disciples left their homes and their jobs to be with Jesus and listen to what He taught. They went with Jesus and lived together with Him for three years as He preached, healed, and helped people. Many other people followed Jesus to hear what He said.

Several times Jesus took just the Twelve Disciples and went to special places away from the other people to teach them about God and what God wanted them to do.

After three years, Jesus died on a cross in Jerusalem. The disciples were very sad. They were afraid that the people who killed Jesus would kill them. They were afraid and hid in houses and locked the doors so no one would know they were there. Some of the disciples went back to their jobs and homes away from Jerusalem.

Then Jesus arose from the grave on the first Easter. He appeared to the disciples in different places. They saw that Jesus was alive and Jesus was with them.

Jesus told them, He had to go away from them. He told them, He would be with each of them in spirit all of the time. He told them not to be afraid of anyone because He would be with them.

Jesus told them to go to everyone and tell them what He had taught them so that people everywhere could have happy lives. He promised that He would be with them no matter where they went or what they did.

He told them, He would send the Holy Spirit to them, and that they should go to Jerusalem, to wait for the coming of the Holy Spirit.

The disciples went to Jerusalem as Jesus had told them, and they waited for the Holy Spirit.

Forty days after Jesus arose from the grave, all of the disciples were in one room. Suddenly a wind blew through the room. Each of the disciples felt the power of the Holy Spirit go through their bodies, minds and spirits. It was like flames of fire going through them but they were not hurt.

They were not afraid of anything anymore. They went out to preach to the people who put Jesus to death. A miracle happened!

There were people in Jerusalem at that time from many different countries. They spoke many different languages.

A miracle happened when the disciples began preaching to all of these different people. Each person heard what the disciples said in their own language.

We call this day, Pentecost. Every year we celebrate the day when the Holy Spirit came to the disciples, just like we celebrate Christmas, when Jesus was born.

At that time, the Apostle Peter preached a sermon, and 3000 people believed that Jesus was the Messiah. They said they would follow the life and teachings of Jesus and do what God wanted them to do.

The Apostles baptized the 3000 people and continued to teach them about Jesus and God. The Apostles knew that they would have to find a way to teach and help them.

In the Book of Acts in the Bible, we read that the Apostles taught the people every day. They sang songs and prayed. This was the first church.

The Apostles chose seven men to take care of setting up the meetings and helping people who needed help. They called them deacons. Stephen was one of the first deacons.

At the same time the enemies of Jesus were trying to stop the Apostles and the people who were with them from following the teachings of Jesus.

They caught Stephen and asked him to stop being a follower of Jesus. Stephen said he would not stop being a follower of Jesus. The enemies of Jesus decided to kill Stephen. They took Stephen outside the city and began throwing stones at him.

Saul, a young man who was a leader of the enemies of Jesus, held the coats of the men who were stoning Stephen.

Then something happened!

As Stephen was dying, he asked Jesus to take his spirit. Then he asked God to forgive the men who were stoning him. Saul saw this and he could not forget the way Stephen forgave the men who were killing him. But Saul still wanted to stop the followers of Jesus.

Saul decided to go to the city of Damascus to arrest more of the followers of Jesus and bring them back to Jerusalem to punish them.

As Saul was walking to Damascus, a bright light in the sky blinded him. He fell to the ground. He heard a voice say, *"Saul, Saul why do you persecute me?"* (Acts 9:4)

Saul said, *"Who are you?"* (Acts 9:5,6)

The voice said, *"I am Jesus whom you persecute. Get up and go to Damascus."* (Acts 9:5)

For three days, Saul could not see. His friends led him to Damascus. A follower of Jesus came to him and healed him. Saul could see again.

Saul became a follower of Jesus. He was baptized. He changed his name from Saul to Paul.

After three years of study in the desert, Paul began to preach and teach about Jesus in many countries. Everywhere Paul traveled, groups of people who believed in Jesus as their savior, formed churches.

At a church in the city of Antioch, the followers of Jesus were first called "Christians." From that time on, churches were called Christian Churches.

Paul wrote many letters to the different churches to help them do what God wanted them to do. His letters are called epistles in the Bible.

The churches usually met to worship on Sundays because it was Sunday when Jesus rose from the grave on the first Easter.

The people in the churches would sing songs of praise to God. They would read the Bible and pray. They would listen to someone explain what the scripture meant.

Each church had a leader who became known as Pastor, like our pastors today. They also had men who helped the pastors. They were called Elders or Deacons.

When a person wanted to become a Christian, the pastor would teach the person about Jesus and God. The person would accept God into their heart and promise to follow the teachings of Jesus. Then the pastor would baptize the person.

Churches were begun by the Apostles of Jesus in many countries to help people everywhere know about God, the life and teachings of Jesus, and the Holy Spirit.

Churches usually have pastors who may be called Ministers or Reverends. They lead, preach, and teach the people. They baptize people who want to become Christians. They also lead Worship and Communion Services.

Churches have men and women who help the pastor. In some churches, they are called Elders or Deacons.

Other people that help churches teach Sunday or Church School classes, sing in the choir and do other things to help the church like visit the sick and take care of the church buildings and business problems.

The church is made up of people, not buildings. They come together to worship God every Sunday and to receive strength to live their lives. It is a good place to learn more about God with friends and neighbors. The church helps us to make good friends with people who love God the way that we love God.

Church members are always trying to help other people. They invite other people to come to church to learn about God.

(After completing this course, a pastor can explain the specific teachings of his or her church.)

# About the Author

Richard B. Hayward, a Presbyterian (USA) retired Air Force Chaplain and pastor has been an evangelism innovator throughout his ministry. Since there were 1200 more ministers than churches when he retired from the Air Force, he completed a year of graduate study in public relations and became a 10 year professional public relations director for all of the YMCAs of San Diego County.

A church in a multicultural urban community was scheduled to be closed in 1988. The members were told it was going to happen. They began praying for someone to help them and Pastor Hayward was praying for some place to serve in a church. God brought them together but no one told Pastor Hayward it was to be closed. He became their pastor and 20 years later he retired.

In his book, he outlines the step by step process of how God and public relations methods helped him and the members continue to minister to people in this challenging situation. He wants to share with other pastors some suggestions to help their churches with some new and innovative ideas to reach the unchurched in their communities for God.

During his Air Force Chaplaincy Career, he ministered to people of all denominations, and since dedicated Christians went to their denominational churches in the nearby towns, he had to develop innovative programs to have a dynamic chapel program on the base.

Some of these included: changing the time of the Sunday Service to increase attendance by 300%; establishing a Protestant Church with a civilian pastor for embassy and other Americans in a foreign country as part of his official duties to provide monthly services; creating a taped radio ministry on a commercial radio station to reach the unchurched all over the state from a top secret base that wouldn't allow visitors; beginning a daily recorded devotional ministry over a hospital radio station for the 300 patients; increasing a youth program from a small group to over 100 young people who met on Sunday nights; originated one of the first Ecumenical Services in the Air Force including Catholic, Protestant and Jewish clergy, choirs, and people; filmed the first promotional film used world-wide to promote Air Force Spiritual Life Conferences; developed daily "Bus Devotionals" with a chaplain on board to bring a message of inspiration while flight line airmen were refreshed with a cool drink and refreshments in the 100 degree heat during the Vietnam War; and produced weekly thirty minute radio programs to encourage people to attend the chapel service of their choice over Armed Forces radio stations for eight years.

During his Air Force Chaplaincy career, he baptized 355 adults, connecting them to civilian churches.

After his Air Force career, in addition to his 10 year award winning professional public relations director career, he became a chaplain-counselor for the Salvation Army Adult Rehabilitation Center in San Diego helping recovering alcoholics for six years and completed 20 years as a pastor.

He originated the DIAL HOPE Telephone Outreach Ministry with daily devotionals and invitations to request prayer and come to church. His church had 55,000 calls with 5,000 requests for prayer during a 10 year period. He wrote and published a <u>DIAL HOPE Manual</u> to help other churches set up their own telephone ministries. Churches in 35 states and Canada have the <u>DIAL HOPE Manual</u> with a potential of 500,000 calls and 50,000 prayer requests annually. (The <u>DIAL HOPE Manual</u> is included in his book.)

Now he wants to share some of his evangelism suggestions with pastors to help them and their churches with renewal, growth and outreach.